Life. Business.
Just got

Brad Burton

@BradBurton

CAPSTONE
A Wiley Brand

This edition first published in 2013
© 2013 Brad Burton

Registered office
Capstone Publishing Ltd. (A Wiley Company), John Wiley and Sons Ltd, The Atrium,
Southern Gate, Chichester, West Sussex, PO19 8SQ, United Kingdom

For details of our global editorial offices, for customer services and for information
about how to apply for permission to reuse the copyright material in this book please
see our website at www.wiley.com.

The right of the author to be identified as the author of this work has been asserted in
accordance with the Copyright, Designs and Patents Act 1988.

Wiley publishes in a variety of print and electronic formats and by print-on-demand.
Some material included with standard print versions of this book may not be included
in e-books or in print-on-demand. If this book refers to media such as a CD or DVD
that is not included in the version you purchased, you may download this material at
http://booksupport.wiley.com. For more information about Wiley products, visit www.
wiley.com.

Designations used by companies to distinguish their products are often claimed as
trademarks. All brand names and product names used in this book and on its cover are
trade names, service marks, trademark or registered trademarks of their respective
owners. The publisher and the book are not associated with any product or vendor
mentioned in this book. None of the companies referenced within the book have
endorsed the book.

Limit of Liability/Disclaimer of Warranty: While the publisher and author have used
their best efforts in preparing this book, they make no representations or warranties
with the respect to the accuracy or completeness of the contents of this book and
specifically disclaim any implied warranties of merchantability or fitness for a particular
purpose. It is sold on the understanding that the publisher is not engaged in rendering
professional services and neither the publisher nor the author shall be liable for
damages arising herefrom. If professional advice or other expert assistance is required,
the services of a competent professional should be sought.

Library of Congress Cataloging-in-Publication Data

Burton, Brad, 1973–
    Life. business. just got easier / Brad Burton.
        pages cm
    ISBN 978-0-857-08483-5 (pbk.)
1. Small business—Management.   2. Decision making.   3. Leadership.   4. Burton,
Brad, 1973– I. Title.
    HD62.7.B847 2013
    658.02'2—dc23   2013018238

A catalogue record for this book is available from the British Library.

ISBN 978–0–857–08483–5 (paperback)   ISBN 978–0–857–08476–7 (ebk)
ISBN 978–0–857–08481–1 (ebk)

Cover design: Mackerel Ltd

Set in 10/13pt Stone by Toppan Best-set Premedia Limited, Hong Kong
Printed in Great Britain by TJ International Ltd, Padstow, Cornwall, UK

DEDICATED TO

Wifey. B.b.D.

*All those, who never gave up on me,
especially my mum and dad 'Frank'.*

@DetectiveDenise never forgotten kiddo. x

Help Many.
Hurt Few.
Live Life.
Braddism

Contents

Foreword   vii

#Justgoteasierbook   xi

1 – The day it all changed   1

2 – Leaders make decisions. Decisions don't make a leader.   19

3 – Two-year plan. Forget it.   31

4 – No passion. No point.   45

5 – The day it all changed for you   59

6 – Win some. Lose none.   73

7 – Eject. Eject. Eject.   87

8 – Jenga!   101

9 – Buy my stuff/never trust a skint telemarketer   115

10 – It's only an ambush if you don't know it's there   129

11 – We lose so many todays worrying about tomorrow   143

12 – Build it and they will come. Sometimes.   155

13 – Experience is what you win, when you lose   173

14 – Sun will shine   187

About Brad Burton   199

Business blah blah blah   201

Acknowledgements   203

Foreword

I've spent much of my career as a main board Director of PLCs. In that time I've seen some huge changes in the way business is conducted in the UK particularly concerning updates in technology, attitudes to dress, the constantly changing economy and people's feelings on work and authority.

I've known Brad for the last seven years, firstly as a member of 4Networking before becoming a Director in 2007 and now at 62, Chairman.

In recent years, Brad has been ahead of any curve and as such resisted by those who would prefer to keep business in the past and in their comfort zone. Brad's demise as a businessman has been predicted just as regularly as his achievements have been denounced and ridiculed.

But his achievements can no longer be claimed to be a fluke, as he has seemingly been in the right place at the right time, *for the last eight years*.

At his best, he brings energy and vision, a driver with a clear focus on problem solving, often seeing the solution to any situation well before others even recognise there is a situation. A gift very few possess.

Whilst others may go around the houses, Brad has gone through your front door and out the back. Without stealing your telly. But things may have been different; from his council estate upbringing, he has changed his future.

He made things happen.

The ridiculous thing is that had he approached me for a position during my "corporate" career, I would have turned him down.

I would have recognised immediately that he would not (and probably could not) have played the politics needed to get on within a traditional business and would have, at the earliest opportunity, wanted to break the mould and do it his way.

That's the reason he started his own business.

He's largely unemployable, true entrepreneurs often are.

He brings such a wide and varied experience of life. Some will say he appears to be at times an intimidating character. Nothing could be further from the truth. He is emotionally hooked up to the world and will go out of his way to take on what he sees to be injustices in life and business, and fight for the underdog.

I've seen top-class negotiators underestimate him. And sit there afterwards scratching their heads as to why it's not gone their way.

I've seen him at his most confident, I've supported him at his very lowest.

At worst he can get too impatient too quickly, switch off just a bit too soon. But he recognises he is as flawed as any human and understands the importance of team and has surrounded himself with people he likes, knows and trusts.

This book is a culmination of his unique thinking on life and business, and if you start by reading this book with an open mind, it may well change your direction, in the same way I've seen his words and teachings change so many.

Including me . . . he's taught this old dog some new tricks and helped steer the way I see today's business world.

Anyone want to buy 30 years of ties?

When things are good, you see what a person stands for, when things are really bad and they are up against the wall, that's when you see how much resolve and belief someone really has.

Is this a book that will change your life/business?

You will soon find out.

@4NTerryCooper
Chairman/4Networking Limited

#Justgoteasierbook

At the time of writing I've tweeted over 150,000 times, amassed 100,000+ followers, so it's fair to say I'm a pretty active tweeter. When I'm on the road it keeps me focused, amused, busy; it's like having my friends in my pocket.

And as you read through this book, you can also join me on that journey. At the end of each chapter you will come across a # hashtag (think of them like filing cabinets for Twitter), as you read this ping me a relevant tweet, feedback, photo, whatever, I'll aim at responding to as many as I sensibly can. It's a bit of a novel idea or is that a modern self-help book idea?

Anyway do @BradBurton me with your thoughts, what is relevant to you, and any breakthroughs and feedback.

www.Twitter.com let's connect today.

1

THE DAY
IT ALL
CHANGED

I was a seven-year-old boy, playing *Space Lego* in the front room of our terraced house in Salford, Manchester, whilst my stepdad watched the snooker finals. Suddenly the match went off and the BBC NEWS FLASH title appeared on screen. It switched the coverage over to the Iranian Embassy siege, where a hostage situation was coming to a dramatic and violent ending and for the first time in history the SAS were unveiled to the world's media.

That's when life first changed for me, and I realised that the world I'd been ushered through, the reality I lived in, wasn't in fact *real*.

Up until that point I was quite rightly led to believe it was all *Tiswas*, toys, Father Christmas and *Beano* comics.

Most good parents are masterful at creating a faux environment, to allow kids to hang onto childhood for as long as possible. This makes children feel safe and secure while they do their learning about the real world . . .

I'm about to bombshell you.

The grown-up world in which you currently exist is most likely also not the one you have been led to believe it is by government, society, magazines, the powers that be.

- A **job for life**
- **Work hard** and you'll get yours.
- You'll retire when you're 65 with a **comfortable pension**.
- **Trusty** bank manager

We hang onto that because it feels safe.

Then we get to the end of our life, only to realise that the rules we've been playing by may have been the wrong ones.

Why wait a lifetime for that realisation?

The penny dropped for me a few years ago when I realised that the only guarantee in life . . .

. . . Was for its duration, is that you've got one.

What's stopping you living the life that you really want?

The truth is . . . It's probably you.

You may believe you don't have the skills, qualifications, the finance or simply what it takes, to have the life you want.

If you *believe* that, you are absolutely right.

So maybe the key to this is to start believing that you *do* have exactly what is needed to make the life you want happen.

Perhaps your goals seem so far over the horizon that they appear to be practically impossible and as a result *what's the point*, and so you don't get round to starting.

You just kind of . . . drift, with the days, months and years passing and before you know it, it's years of regret and what ifs.

But, before we move onto that, maybe I've got it wrong. Perhaps you've already got the life you do actually want.

Providing you're not in a public place, I want you to, without any hesitation, quickly answer this next question out loud:

What my life needs more of is _____
(say it or think it <LOUD>)

What was the first thing you thought of?

Is what you said _really_ lacking?

If what immediately springs to mind was addressed and fixed, is it fair to assume that this would indeed make your Life and Business that little bit easier?

What you'll discover throughout this book are lessons, words and stories, all written to show you a way through whatever is going on in your life/business.

These stories will stay with you and accompany you on your pathway towards YOUR goal.

None of this is about being mercenary or in any way needing to walk over people to get it. It's about finding within yourself that sweet spot, the balance between pace and progress while all the time retaining control and not unravelling.

This is a book that will change your thinking, change your direction, change your life.

Change YOU.

To a greater or lesser degree we all hide the truth to the world about who we _really_ are and I see this heightened in a business capacity. We put on show, a version of ourselves to the world, because sometimes it's easier that way. It may be at first, but this can undermine your clarity and short circuit your own thinking as to who you are and what you stand for.

Right now there is just me and you, because no one else is reading this with you. So, throughout this book I want you to be really honest with yourself about your situation. Be honest about the little steps you are going to need to take (lots of them) in order to get yourself the life you want.

We are going to cover the lessons I've picked up and learnt along the way since I wrote my previous books *Get Off Your Arse* and *Get Off Your Arse Too*.

We'll be mixing business and pleasure, as I've checked with the publisher and we do have a laughing and smiling and AHA! licence in place.

You are going to enjoy this book.

Third book eh, so it's a bit like *Return of the Jedi*, but with no Ewoks (even though I rather like them . . .).

The first book was my *Star Wars*, something genuinely new that seemed to come out of nowhere. Although, if I'm honest, I didn't really know what it was. It's a mish-mash of networking, life and business all rolled into one, and in my business naivety I felt it would work and you know what? It did.

I'd accidentally carved out a niche. A unique approach within the personal development/business genre. It caused bookstore managers all manner of headaches as to which area it should be displayed in.

Self-help section or is it business? The lessons overlapped. Because I know from experience, **if your head isn't right, your business isn't right.**

Just because something doesn't have an existing label, doesn't mean it won't work.

Get Off Your Arse Too, like *The Empire Strikes Back*, was darker, as I shared the worst day of my life, not to be dramatic, but for two reasons. One for you the reader to understand that your past doesn't need to steal your future and secondly (which I didn't reveal at the time) as an insurance policy. As my profile is increasing I'd rather get that story out there so it can't be used against me when I become the next Dragon!

I'm joking.

Kind of.

So in some respects it was there as an insurance – if something was to happen to me, it's documented. That chapter of my life is behind me.

I have complete conviction that this book will turn on lightbulbs within you.

Illuminating a way forward for you.

Here you will find the most recent stories I've amassed. I now know what I'm looking for – interesting characters I've met and lessons I've picked up through my now, veteran eyes, all weaved into business, business into life.

One thing that has come through loud and clear is that I'm not Superman and that even with the ra ra motivational stuff, I have my own hang-ups and fears.

You probably do too, but that's OK. Why? Because you are normal.

But I have learned something very valuable . . .

That nearly every negative can be turned into a genuine positive.

For people new to one of my books, I'm the MD/founder of a national business networking organisation, 4Networking (www.4networking.biz), which offers a unique approach to networking through the 5,000 events we run each year across the UK blah blah blah.

Sales pitch over and I won't mention it again. OK, that's not strictly true, but I'll aim to keep the references to a minimum.

No qualifications. £25k of personal debt when I started my first marketing biz. Ended up having to deliver pizzas to stay afloat.

Back then, I was skint, as in really skint. A friend of mine, Jay, who was relatively well off with his highly paid corporate job, would bung me a few quid to help me out every time he visited, and I always remember he wore this amazing watch, a Rado.

I'd ask him if I could wear it. On my wrist it just blinged. I could see me having one of those one day, when I had made it.

Ten years later, the day arrived when I actually had the money I needed to buy one, so I drove to the jewellers at shopping centre where I had window shopped so many times in previous years.

This jewellers was an Authorised Rado Stockist. So no cheap knock-offs at this place.

For the first time in my life I had the cash in my pocket to buy my dream watch. The shop assistant came over and asked me, "Which of the Rados do you most like?" Clever.

I couldn't make my mind up.

Was it the pure black one with the diamond at the 12 o'clock position or the black and silver one, or the black and gold?

Decisions, decisions.

Then I had this epiphany, a realisation . . .

I didn't actually want a friggin' Rado watch anymore!

It had been the thrill of the chase. Wanting what you can't have. The magic of that watch fell away right then and there in the shop. I told the bloke that I'd have a walk around and think about it.

I did walk around and think about it and my thoughts remained the same.

See, that car/handbag/desirable thing that you've been hankering after is just no longer as important or attractive when you can afford it.

Ever since being a young boy and having a *Countach* poster and seeing one on *Smokey and the Bandit*, I'd always conformed to being male and had wanted a Lamborghini.

But I'm reliably told that the only two days' enjoyment you get from a supercar are the day you buy it and the day you sell it.

When I first started my business, I saw a speaker at a seminar gush about the power of a "dream board" and all the start-up business attendees furiously scribbled down this idea.

That evening, cork boards, full of inspirational quotes and pictures from magazines of dream houses were hung up in home offices across the land.

If you've ever done that, sorry to be a bit harsh, but **put away the scissors and pins and do something more constructive to move you towards your goal.**

Having dreams is essential. But wasting time incessantly dreaming takes you further away from them becoming a reality.

In life, there are talkers and doers and I'm both.

What are you?

It's just you and me here, so you can be totally honest with yourself.

It ain't going to happen unless you, yes YOU, make it happen.

My outrageous goal was to create a national business network. We achieved that and are now moving on to actively change the entire UK SME business scene.

In some respects, having reached my seemingly impossible goal, what now?

It's a bit like a youngster, who looks at photos of Everest and spends their life dreaming about the moment when they scale it. Then, as an adult having spent seven years training and two weeks climbing to the summit and taking in the breathtaking vista . . .

And then the penny drops. It's just a friggin' mountain.

People like Mike Tyson, who became heavyweight champion of the world and then his world fell apart. No longer any goal, no longer any direction.

Once your seemingly insurmountable goals have been reached, then what?

I now head up a multi-million pound international business created within seven years.

Those are my credentials.

Over the last few years I've also become a major motivational business speaker. Speaking at major UK business shows and high fiving the MDs of the big companies I'm booked by. It's my sweary, brash, no-nonsense approach to business and my trademark jeans, trainers and T-shirt approach when presenting that they love. Probably.

And then I get involved with business journeys like this, which highlight just why I love doing this . . . I'll let Chrissie introduce the situation to you:

"I met with Brad at a networking event around four months into setting up my own business. I had a 10-minute chat with him as I knew that he had started 4Networking without a big cash injection and I had started my own recruitment business in a similar way".

I then asked her the question, "How do you know if the way you are running your business is right?"

Chrissie said, "I'm knackered and I work ridiculous hours but love what I do".

My reply was, "Have you read my book?"

"No."

"Read my book, as it will help you to answer my question about the way you are running your business, and a lot more besides. Not everyone is cut out to be self-employed, but the best thing about it is that you get to choose which 18 hours a day you work! Just read my book."

"OK yes, I will, thanks Brad."

A few months later I received an email:

Hi Brad,

Hope you're well,

Just wanting some words of inspiration from you.

Between you and me my business is 8 months old and the money is still not coming in at the level it should be to cover bills etc.

Recruitment is a tough business, because the time from an initial meeting to gaining business and placing a candidate and then getting paid is at least 3 months.

As a result, I am getting very frustrated. How did you keep going?

I am very confident in my ability and I know this business will work, but I just need to get over this initial struggle and find a way of getting back my *va va voom*.

I've felt flat this week and I can tell that people around me don't have the faith they had at the beginning.

xxxxxx

The second I'd finished the email I picked up the phone – "Hiya Chrissie, did you read my book after we spoke?"

"No."

"For f*ck's sake C, if you'd bought the book we wouldn't be having this conversation now! This isn't about me making £1.27 out of the book – this is about you sorting your biz out. Read both books, then let's talk."

*click

Chrissie has since described what happened next:

"I bought both *GOYA* books. They changed my way of thinking. I don't go for 'self-help' books that people rave about, which is why I didn't get Brad's books in the first place. I'd thought they would be the 'same old self-help stuff' and that Brad was just trying to sell me his book!

Some time later I met Brad at a business show and I was thrilled to be able to tell him that I'd recently won a *New Business of the Year* award. He was genuinely delighted for me.

I go back to Brad's books every now and then for a pick-me-up. They're not self-help books, they are reality-check books, written by a real person for real people."

Which brings me nicely onto @GeorgeSavva1, who heads up the communications company 7 Seconds. He had this to say on this subject:

"It's classic car owner's manual syndrome. Most people believe that they don't need to read their car owner's manual because they know how to drive. This is foolhardy because most of the car's unknown true potential is revealed in that manual.

Just by reading it, you can find out how to get the best from your car.

Networking is not dissimilar. How many people go networking and never take the trouble to read a book or two on how to do it properly?

I find it amazing that when it comes to getting the best out of 4Networking, how few people have ever read Brad's first book, let alone the second. This is significant because people can and do make judgement calls on the effectiveness of networking, never ever taking the time to learn how to do it effectively! This is tantamount to labelling the car as useless because you failed to put diesel in the tank! If you want to get moving, you have to take the first logical step!"

The above isn't put in to talk about how clever I am, or a *stealth* plug to buy my books. It's about how the answer you are looking for is sometimes right in front of your nose, your bookshelf or even already within you, yet we choose to ignore it because we are sceptical or unbelieving.

I was 32 when I started my first business – I'd done years on the dole, and had my windows shot through when I was 21 years old. I think it's fair to say I'd found myself on the wrong side of the tracks, but I'm still that same guy. The difference is I changed direction. I changed tracks.

I. I. I.

Me. Me. Me.

It hasn't been easy. Far from it. Changing from a street-smart kid to a Wiley businessman. The reason difficult changes are called difficult changes is, well the clue is in the words "difficult changes".

They are painful. You'll question whether you are making the right call. Why? Because they are d i f f i c u l t.

In order for things to change, things need to change.

I'm going to be talking directly to you throughout this book. It's not all about Me. It's about You and Me.

You will already have all the ingredients you need for success, for being the best you can be. Absolutely true.

Whether at this moment in time you've quite got the recipe right is something only you can answer, but over the course of this book, we, that is me and you together, are going to coax that recipe out of you.

Your recipe.

You up for it?

As in really up for it? If not, put the book down and walk away. Spend the time on something you would prefer to do. Ideally pass this book to someone who *is* up for it.

I'm talking to you.

You've stayed with me this far, so maybe the time for you to make changes is NOW. Take a moment to **find that button within you, the one that says yeah, SUCCESS MODE ON.**

Press it.

Well done you.

Throughout the course of the next 13 chapters it's going to get interesting.

Some of the things I write may not make immediate sense to you – you may think, what's the lesson??! But later on you'll be driving along and all of a sudden it will come to you, you will just get it.

Digest the lessons and understand that every single word in this is aimed at helping you with your life, with your business.

I've downloaded my brain into this book.

People only worry about their work/life balance if they don't enjoy their job.

So what have you learned?

LIFE:

BUSINESS:

IDEAS:

Is your life/business likely to be that little bit easier? Y / N

2

LEADERS MAKE DECISIONS. DECISIONS DON'T MAKE A LEADER.

When you are finding your feet as a leader, it's tough at the top, but it's even tougher at the bottom.

One of the best things about running your own business is that you can't get fired from it!

Well technically you can if you lose control, but if you've lost control, it's no longer your business. So always maintain control.

This doesn't mean you can't bring people in to support you, or not trust anyone. But do ensure that those who are coming on the journey actually want to be on *your* journey.

Think of it a bit like the *Wizard of Oz*. Everyone has a reason for coming along, and so they should, but the last thing you want is the Wicked Witch tagging along.

What does or would being your own boss mean to you?

For me it means I can truly be myself. In business, what's so radical about being 100% you, 100% of the time?

Being a business owner means others have to play to your rules rather than you toeing someone else's company line.

For me at the very least it means I can go to the gym most days in, dare I say it, *work* hours, often doing #selfies along the way. Have a look for yourself at http://instagram.com/BradBurton. How the hell people manage to work and juggle family commitments whilst working to set hours is beyond me.

In those first few years self-employment is often just a real day-to-day struggle, with plenty of sacrifices along the way. But as time goes on you need to work towards developing a role that perfectly fits your skills and strengths. You'll know you've achieved that when you hit the sweet spot of enjoying every moment of your work, so much so that it doesn't actually feel like *real work*.

I'm always working. I'm always resting.

If you get it right, you'll become unemployable. I certainly am.

More than that, having recently got a big lion/eagle tattoo on each forearm, I've made my *burn the bridges* strategy a little more real. I now really do have to make my plan work.

My tattoos make me unique and marketable, on so many fronts. Well that's the story I tell myself, as in fact the visit to the tattoo parlour was probably a pre-mid-life crisis moment. When you run your own business and run your own life, you can do daft things like that.

You don't have to be a prisoner to the conventional, the normal. Your only judge should be your sales, growth and business results. Don't try to be something you're not as it's too hard to maintain consistency at not being yourself.

Play to your strengths, hire to your weaknesses.

Life. Business. Just got easier.

The whole purpose of being your own boss is that it's ultimately down to you. The direction of your business and your future.

The flip-side though is that you no longer have any place to hide. The buck stops with you. You can still go and skive in the loo texting your mates, but it's nowhere near as much fun as when you were employed and got paid for wasting time.

Your team should march to the beat of your drum or they should find their happiness elsewhere. But maybe you have no team just yet, that's ok because . . .

To start a business, you only need three things – a mobile phone, shoe leather and BIG balls!

To be a successful leader you need to add another three things:

An idea, vision and belief.

Calling yourself a leader doesn't make you a leader. The way you lead is by making decisions. The more decisions you make that end up after the event being viewed as the correct ones, generally shows that you are becoming a better leader.

Here's the drill I use to mentor people, to help them to make important calls and fast . . .

Consider all the options.

Is there a significant risk?

What will you accomplish if this works? Can you live with the outcome if it doesn't go your way? In my experience people who make slow decisions make as many BIG bad decisions as people who make fast ones. Make fast decisions.

As you get nearer to the decision you should get more confident not less. *How do you eat a pizza?*

Personally I start with the piece with the most topping. Slice by slice is the key. Otherwise you end up making a mess. That exact same principle can be used for any call you have to make. Divide it up into bite-sized chunks, so that you can see your choices more clearly.

You can never truly be your own boss until you stop living your life through the filter of other people's opinions. If you believe something will work, try it. If it doesn't, you've learned something.

Remember, you are the boss. Success or failure, that's down to you. A daft approach is only daft if it doesn't work. The cheapest and most powerful business tool you have is your brain so always use that first. By all means take advice, but constantly looking to others for approval is pointless. Your business is nobody's but your own.

You are a leader. Even if the only person you currently lead is yourself. You are going to have to be self-motivated, with your actions fuelled by your own intentions and goals.

If you're a loudmouth, sweary northerner who makes things happen, be consistent, so that people know exactly what you're about.

Make the most of what you've got.

Some people don't want to have their own business. Instead they want to be led. I picked up on my Twitter feed someone local to me who was looking for a job.

#HelpGetBarneyAJob

I replied, "Barney, why waste time looking for a job when you can start your own job today and begin looking for clients? Email me your details and I'll send you my books. I'll also take you out for some lunch and see if I can assist you in starting your own biz".

"Thanks Brad, that'd be amazing."

He never did send me the email.

Six weeks on he's still banging on Twitter with #HelpGet-BarneyAJob. I heard him on the radio – he just did an 80-mile round trip for a radio interview to talk about his Twitter campaign and *plight*, but as a result of his *intensive job search*, he never quite found the time to send the email he promised me, nor drive the seven minutes for the free lunch.

The comedic irony of all this is that I had a potential job for him within my business. Absolutely true. Yet because he never did what *he said* he would, he failed the first part of my stealth interview process. He deselected himself.

Be honest with yourself.

Not everyone is cut out for self-employment. It can be the best of times, the worst of times.

Neil and Tracey, a husband and wife team from the small hall events company Sterling Integrity, recounted a story of how in 1994 they had all the trappings of success, running a construction company with 20 staff and a lovely office. Both of them had matching BMWs on the drive and a beautiful four-bedroom house with double garage. But come the end of the month, after they had paid all the staff wages, they couldn't afford a portion of fish and chips *between* them.

Welcome to running your own business. You'll get your arsed kicked for a while, but then you'll come bouncing back. That's how it is, providing you have the tenacity to keep coming back after a shoeing. To not lose your dream you may have to lose some sleep, and sometimes everyone gets paid except you.

Living the dream. There is a long way to go, right from the minute you believe you can't go on.

Although you can't get fired from your own business, at times you can certainly want to walk away. It can be a very lonely place.

Maybe the biggest change you need to undertake is not to your business, but to your thinking.

The modern leader is fallible and admits mistakes, shares fears, acknowledges faults and in doing so displays a lot of courage. The modern leader is human.

You should ALWAYS try to do right for people and never sell someone something they don't really want, whether it's a product OR a dream.

Regardless of what people may think of you or your methods, be a wo/man of your word. Say what you mean, mean what you say. None of us are perfect, but as long as your intentions are always the right ones . . . Why wait? With anything in your life, if you are thinking about it, it's probably an indicator that you ought to do something about it. Even if the only thing you do is acknowledge that you must do something about it next week.

When you're feeling strong, your decisions become laser focused and sniper-like in their accuracy. But when your resolve is weaker, those are the days when your thinking is muddy. So, ensure you only make important decisions when you're feeling on top of things.

You are going to have to make calls that no-one else can do for you – it's going to be YOUR decision. So own it and be brave enough to do so.

Decision making can be like being that sniper and having a target in your sights. Just at the point you are going to pull the trigger an overwhelming inner voice says *no, no, no* and before you know it, your certainty has fallen away, replaced with fear, apprehension and anxiety. You've missed your moment, the target has moved out of your sights and you don't have the courage to take the decision anymore just in case of X or Y.

At some point you are going to have to pull the trigger.

Take the shot, rather than constant adjustment and re-adjustment. The only time you will know if you've made the right decision is after the event.

As you can't get fired from your own business, you can make calls that people say you shouldn't. If they don't work out, so what? NEXT. If they do, you are a strategic genius. Sometimes there is no right answer, but not making a decision, that's always the wrong answer. Wait too long and the opportunity that presented itself to you is wasted. If you are your own boss, you can't be gun shy.

At times, you will find yourself in a lonely, downward, negative spiral, wasting energy. You'll be going nowhere or making little progress.

At that point, take a break from people, go walk the dog, walk on the beach, sit in a park, take stock of your life and what you stand for.

Successful leaders focus on things that matter and surround themselves with smart people.

Take a moment to think about the five adults who share your life. ***These people will be affecting your business, your relationships, your whole life.***

Those people are your circle of influence – you rely on them for support and encouragement, words of wisdom and love. Do they meet your needs?

Are these people and relationships empowering, enriching, adding stability, moving you towards your goals? Or are they toxic, poisoning your resolve, eroding your strength and making you feel defeated? If the people in your circle of influence make you feel like shit, weaken or disempower you, then you need to look at changing your circle of influence.

However that circle is making you feel will be the total sum of your results. Resistance or assistance.

You can't hold onto everyone and you're not meant to. People leave so new people can arrive.

It's tough at the top, as decisions can't be avoided. But you should seek advice and a sounding board from those you trust. Your ability to handle pressure will be crucial. Remember, there's no hiding place. If you worry too much, it'll start to show. Overload causes anxiety, anxiety causes panic, panicking leaders cause panicking staff.

Think about those times at a supermarket self-service checkout, when something just won't scan. You can keep trying the same swipe but all you will achieve is frustration and a log jam. Plus you begin to become conscious of the people behind you, who have now started tutting and rolling their eyes. Causing you to repeat the same action that didn't work the first time, but faster . . .

Walk away from a situation, get some head space and then come back to it.

Be clear, get a plan and do something. You only need a loose plan. Move towards it. You can do this. **Set your emotional clock to forward. To a brighter day.**

If things are really not working out with something, change it, change it, change it. Until it does work. The key to doing this is to just keep moving. Be content with small incremental gains instead of trying to grab big gulps of ground and then, each and every day you will make progress.

Align yourself with a team of dreamers, thinkers, doers and believers. Move away from the haters, critics and blamers.

Always be even-handed, fair and approachable. Be the leader that others want to follow. Surround yourself with a team which shares your values, your vision, your belief.

If you get your own business right, it becomes about a whole lot more than making money – it starts to make a difference to everyone who is prepared to go on your adventure.

If you lose hope, you lose the fight.

So what have you learned?

LIFE:

BUSINESS:

IDEAS:

Is your life/business likely to be that little bit easier? Y / N

3

TWO-YEAR PLAN. PLAN. FORGET IT.

So many business people get wrapped up in doing *business-like activity*. Stuff that adds little actual value to their business. It's what I used to do back in the bad old days of corporate life. Worrying about whether it's B2B or B2C, when in reality it's B2P. People. Business is that simple.

It's less to do with business, it's all to do with people.

I spoke with an aspiring author and we got on to the subject of books and writing. He shared with me the route he had taken to try to get a publishing deal. His approach involved drafting a 100-page book concept overview and proposal.

I said to him, "That's where you are going wrong. Ask yourself this question – if you were the publisher sat opposite you, would your approach work?"

"What do you mean?" he said.

I said, "How many book ideas/approaches do you think major publishers get each day through the post or by email? Let's say conservatively they receive 2 or 3 a day. Would *you* honestly spend hours reading through each 100-page proposal or more likely would you rapidly flick through the first few pages and then ask your PA to send a polite 'thanks, but no thanks' letter?

If you wouldn't read a 100-page proposal, then the smart thing to do is to change your approach to something more attention grabbing that WILL work, one that would cause YOU to say 'Yes'. Your priorities are not others' priorities. Always think about things from the viewpoint of the person sat opposite you."

Why waste life on stuff that has little chance of working? Of course it's a numbers game, but so is writing a 192-page book.

Instead of writing the lengthy proposal, write the book!

The proposal I wrote to the publishers behind this book (Wiley), was only 300 words across two sides of A4.

They accepted it.

At no point did I dust off my three-piece suit and visit their swanky London offices (and yes they are swanky), occasionally glancing at my gold-chained pocket watch, with the hours of hard negotiations going back on forth.

I emailed my two-pager and followed up with *a phone call*.

How quaint.

Stop hiding behind emails. Stop hiding behind social media. Ultimately you are going to need to talk to someone about what it is you want that person to know and do.

First one to ring gets the job.

Though the truth is, I'd met this publisher at various events over the last five years. They knew me, I knew them. I had a reputation. I'd already been pretty successfully self-published and that's most likely the reason they wanted this one.

I had a track record. I had a reputation for saying what I'm going to do, and then actually doing it. Plus it helped that we had also maintained a warm relationship.

Ask yourself this question and be completely un-emotive about it – why should someone say yes to you about your offering? Just because you say something is great doesn't mean it *is* great.

I'd built a crowd.

Remember the old "Build it and they will come".

In today's world this will only work if you build something people can't get a better version of elsewhere – we'll cover this in more detail later.

A lesson from my first book: *create the conditions where people buy*.

So, back to the aspiring author. This person was blaming the publishers for not accepting his book(s).

That's right, book(s) – he had written 3×100-page proposals for different books, for different publishers.

In this situation, it's easier for this person to blame the other party, the publishers, by saying things like "they are full of their own importance" or "they've got their heads up their arses."

When maybe it's you that is full of your own importance and has got your head up your own arse.

Ask this question: why do you keep getting Noes instead of Yesses?

Going forward, let's be a bit radical. I was mentoring at a company and I said to the client, "Can I see your business plan?" With supreme confidence the client said, "Sure".

Reaching into that second drawer down on the right the document was fished out from under a sea of business cards they'd hoovered up whilst *networking*.

Blowing away the cobwebs, it was handed to me, I kid you not, an 84-page ring-bound document.

I feigned interest in it as I leafed through each of the EIGHTY-FOUR pages. Then for dramatic effect, I threw it in the bin.

"Hang about, we spent £3,500 on that!"

I said, "Let's be honest here, you've not actually looked at this since the day you produced it for that presentation you needed to make to the bank".

They reluctantly agreed. Just because you've got a business plan doesn't mean you are going to do it.

How do I know that? Because business people don't re-read business plans. Generally they are far too busy doing stuff for the future than looking back over a document that was only relevant months ago.

You don't need to pay handsomely for a six-page social media strategy with your name inserted in place of the previous company the expert sold the same strategy to. Unless of course you are going to actually do the things you are paying for.

Grab your pen, as I'm going to let you have my business plan, the plan that has taken me to where I am currently.

Here it is.

To be better in the next two weeks than the preceding two weeks.

That's it.

Let's call it £500. Is that really such a daft business plan?

As *professional business people* we sometimes get bounced into doing big daft folders of stuff in order to feel *professional*.

Wouldn't that time and money be better spent elsewhere? Only you can truly answer that.

By all means have a plan – you are going to need one. But it doesn't need to be ring-bound and cost thousands of pounds to be effective.

A plan can be in your head, a plan can change, a plan WILL change – it has to.

My current plan is to run 10,000 networking events each year. Only another 4,000 to go.

How I'm going to achieve that is by making sure that every activity I or my team undertakes is likely to INCREASE:

- Membership
- Groups
- Attendance
- Morale
- Fun

If the answer is yes to at least one or preferably more than one of those things, we do it.

If the answer is no, I go and find something that will.

Flip that to your activity, your business, your plan. Every fibre and every waking moment when you are working should be spent in moving you towards achieving your plan.

Does your activity INCREASE:

- Sales
- Reputation
- Morale
- Momentum

In the early 90s, I played a PC game called *Civilization*. You start off as a tribe with spears and then through decisions you make, you end up acquiring better knowledge. You can choose which direction your civilisation/tribe goes in by spending money on farming, schools, weaponry, but it's a balancing act of resource management like all these types of game.

So if you invest in creating a civil defence force, you may not have enough remaining resource to build granaries and so forth.

When I started the game, my vision was to create a wonderfully benign tribe which had the best of intentions, used diplomacy and focused on education and the economy.

This was going really well until all of a sudden from beyond my borders came a small army of horseback raiders. This was the first time I'd encountered aggression and my arable farmers paid a heavy price before finally pushing back these aggressors.

Feeling somewhat scarred from the encounter, I decided that was it, I would ensure my tribe would be prepared should these raiders ever choose to return.

So I diverted resources from farming and spent lots of the money in creating my own horseback army. Then, as the years went by, my civilisation discovered the technology of gunpowder. We began to make muskets and cannons for our soldiers.

Then it struck me. I'm actually going to go and even the score with those murderous raiders. Armed to the teeth, my army headed over to their territory and achieved a near instant win – *peace through superior firepower.*

A massacre.

In doing so, their resources and buildings were now my resources, my buildings, allowing me to make even more muskets, more cannons.

You see where this is going . . .

Easy pickings. I sent my troops further into neighbouring areas and we did the same again and again. More resources. More confidence. More buildings. More weapons.

As the years within the game passed, we had more resources because of the pillaging and eventually I ended up with the equivalent of WW2 tanks.

More pillaging. The excitement of winning took over.

Then something happened.

I moved my battalion of tanks one square too far. I was greeted by a stealth bomber which instantly decimated my, up until this point, previously invincible tanks.

I'm a gamer. I've played thousands of hours over the last 30 odd years, but this particular game resonated with me, but I never actually understood the significance of it until now.

That you can have read every self-help book in the world, have the most beautifully presented business plan, and that's great.

But punch bags don't punch back.

You are going to get stealth bombers in your life, stuff that you don't see coming, but it's knowing what to do in the event of it happening that's important.

Going back to my *Civilization* game, my intention from the outset had been to be a benign leader and after being attacked I took my tribe in a direction which I hadn't set out to.

Things derail our good intentions. Circumstances can overrun our positive direction, our plans.

So, accept that a plan is just that, but that it's likely to go to tatters at some point.

Be prepared to adapt, as sticking rigidly to a plan, especially when it's failing, is not a smart move.

Cards on the table, the truth is that my own organisation lost its way as we, the royal we, became too focused on the BIGGER picture. We couldn't see below that and as a result we missed vital opportunities. Right now the company is rightly back to being focused on the little picture, on getting the details right. If you get hundreds of little pictures right, the big picture paints itself.

You know what a strategy is? It's just a guess, possibly an informed one, but never more than that, regardless of how much you have invested in it. As soon as you recognise that a strategy isn't working, be brave enough to change it.

In a meeting a few years back, the person opposite me said to me with a completely straight face, "But Brad, you are not aligned with your company's [4Networking] vision".

At that point I was too weak to take him to task, but looking back there are so many things I should have said, so many things I could have done.

After all it was my company, I started it, I was member number 1.

Something, somewhere clearly wasn't quite right.

It's a bit like saying to Branson, "Hey Richard, you are not aligned with the Virgin brand".

Laughable isn't it.

Well it may be now, but it wasn't then.

You too are going to find yourself in situations where you have either painted or been painted into a corner and unfortunately getting sticky feet is the only way to get out.

What you need is a loose plan, twinned with an outrageous goal!

That's all I've ever had.

Mission statements are more bullshit for a staffer to get paid for or for a self-employed person to dick about with, flashed up on your iPad, it's dicking about v2.0.

Back to the plan. A plan that works.

Work on having three business trajectories going at all times – short, medium and long. I'm always looking for small quick wins which may be teeny but which keep the momentum going forward and carry you each and every day. Those small wins give you the strength and purpose to keep developing your medium- and long-term trajectories. And, as on a conveyor belt, always keep adding things to your short plan, so that as you complete one, another one takes its place.

Making small, incremental gains, quick wins, allow you to praise yourself, stay motivated and keep driving forward.

Remember this. Real work does not have to feel real like work.

So what have you learned?

LIFE:

BUSINESS:

IDEAS:

Is your life/business likely to be that little bit easier? Y / N

4

NO PASSION.
NO POINT.

If you are dreading Monday mornings or your weekends are going too fast, you are in the wrong job, the wrong business.

As a young lad, bath night was Sunday. I'd get out of the bath and plonk down in front of the electric fire and watch *Last of the Summer Wine*, and then feel that dark cloud of a Monday school day forming . . . ugh, not looking forward to tomorrow.

Your tomorrow, are you looking forward to it?

If not, why not? What is it about "tomorrow" that fills you with such trepidation?

@jonhendo78, Managing Director of Vigilant Security, says, "In the months before I started my own business, I'd get what I called my Sunday night anxiety sleep, filled with dread about having to work another week for a company I no longer wanted to be at. I'd wake up after 8 hours, feeling exhausted and irritable – just what you need to set you up for the work day.

Ha, when I finally did leave my job, my anxiety sleep became spread over 7 nights, caused by no longer having a regular income. But at least it was anxiety I was in control of."

How cool would it be if you looked forward to every day?

Very cool.

There is a small step that you can take right now that heads you towards the life you want.

It starts with addressing something real basic.

Sorry to break it to you, the "conventional" work/life balance is a myth.

But there are things you can do to get balance into your life.

How about not trying to grind out a work day if you can't be arsed working and are not in the right mindset.

Always ask yourself, "Is this the best use of my time?" If not, go do something that is.

You are going to need to be brave enough to go do something more productive with your time.

"I'm running my own business, there really aren't enough hours in the day!"

If you've ever found yourself saying that, here's what I want you to do – every 15 minutes, write down what you've done and after about 1 hour 45 minutes I promise you, most people at the very least, begin to consider writing "dicking about".

Here's another one – at the end of each day, jot down how hard you worked on a scale of 1–10. More often than not you'll find you'll write a 5, which in percentile terms is 50% output.

50% of your output every working week, every month, frittered away, pretending to work.

When you're in CAT-MODE™ and you just can't be bothered working, don't. Walk away from your desk instead of sitting there like a corporate robot, programmed to constantly press f5 between 9am and 5pm, awaiting those responses to your *emailed* proposals.

When you transition from corporate, you are almost mentally chained to your desk between office hours. We've all had those jobs that just linger on your to-do list – they haunt you and when you've run out of excuses or time and have no option other than to finally tackle them, you magically burn through them in about 10 minutes a piece.

@GeorgeSavva1 had this to say on this subject of to-do lists.

"Have you ever noticed how *destructive* they are? You find yourself with a list of 25–30 items, and when you ask yourself the question at the end of the day, 'What did I accomplish today?' you find that it's very little.

That's because to-do lists very quickly become '**Won't be done!**' lists! This is not because you're a bad person or anything like that. It's simply that these long lists become overwhelming and do not sufficiently rate the *order* of priority! The easiest and most effective way to overcome this anomaly is to make a 'To Be Done' list and on that list name no more than six tasks that absolutely have to be done that day. The idea is to make sure that each of the items will actually lead you towards your objectives. Once you have drawn up those six items, make sure that you do the worst one first. Doing this, you render the rest of the day a piece of cake!"

Why make it more difficult for yourself? Go against convention – during my work day, I always wear jeans, trainers and T-shirts.

This means I no longer have to take the time out, twice a month, to drop off and collect my dry cleaning. £37 for dry cleaning two suits, count me out.

As your own boss, your results speak louder than any suit and tie.

To be effective in business, be effective in business.

I save more money by shaving my own head, and more importantly I save the time I used to spend on fortnightly barber appointments. Plus, let's tot up all those poncey hair products I used to buy.

Being bald has its advantages!

I told you I could find the positive in most situations.

So now, I just roll out of bed, have a quick shower, T-shirt, jeans, trainers and I'm good to go.

This is a brave new world and one which you can have a part of. OK not sure jeans, T-shirt and trainers are perhaps a winning look if you're female, but wearing clothes you are comfortable with rather than formal business wear every day may work for you. Boiling this down, are there elements of your current life where you are wasting time, doing things that actually have no real bearing on the direction or success of your life?

I'm *half* joking. But in doing what I do, I probably save four hours a month, that's 48 hours a year to do stuff that is more important. I'm not conforming, but instead I'm taking back wasted hours. Cut stuff that doesn't matter out of your day and replace it with stuff that does.

If you are doing something you don't enjoy, the likelihood is you are going to suck at it.

If you're a sales rep, hiding in a B-road lay-by in your company Astra with a newspaper over your head, mobile phone on divert, burning through the minutes until home time, you're in the wrong job.

Back in 2005, I ran a one-man-band marketing/sales consultancy. I somehow managed to win two days of consultancy at £75 an hour, which was BIG money for me back then.

Four hours in, I realised that I didn't like the people I was working with, or the business itself. My (admittedly low) boredom threshold had already started to kick in and I still had another four hours of work to pretend to do that day.

When I got home that evening, I was filled with anxiety and stress about the following day and this was followed by a sleepless night.

I was facing another eight-hour day to do a job for a company that I knew even they didn't believe in.

At various times in our life, we of course all have to do things for money rather than for passion, and that's how it has to be, but could you do a lifetime of that?

It ends up impacting on your health and wellbeing.

I couldn't do it. I struggled at just 16 hours.

Some work a lifetime in a job they don't enjoy. Worse still are those who live a lifetime in a life they don't enjoy. If you don't like your situation, your surroundings, change it.

Look, sometimes you have no options and just need to suck up whatever job is on your desk and get on and do it. But other times, when you're lacking in any pizzazz, walk away and do something you want to. My Twitter @BradBurton is full of gems just like this, "It's 3pm on a Thursday, I'm in bed, playing Modern Warfare 3. #winning".

Or the great Twitter classic, **"I'm walking the dog. LOL"**

I'll then get responses from "That's not very professional" to "What dog have you got?"

My social media strategy . . . is being myself.

You and you alone should define what is professional or not. Never underestimate the positive value that chit-chat, online or in real life, can have on your business and interests. It's the social glue that holds people together. What we say and how we say it matters, no more importantly than in networking situations.

@GeorgeSavva1, "How often do the large multinational advertisers change their adverts that we're so accustomed to on radio, television or other media? They don't change them often, do they? That's because they recognise that, by and large, those adverts are designed to '*educate*' rather than 'sell'. Your 40-second networking infomercial is no different! Standing up in front of a group of people declaring your name, rank and serial number does nothing for a person who is about to take the next bite of his breakfast, lunch or dinner. You have a great deal of competition to contend with at a networking meeting and the effectiveness of your infomercial will depend on the degree to which you make it *applicable to the listener*. The starting point is to recognise that the reason you're at the meeting is to *create advocates* in the fullness of time. You do so by teaching people how to represent YOU when they uncover an opportunity".

Everything speaks about what you do and if you don't have real passion for what you do, certainly in business, it's going to come down to price or personality.

That's OK, if you are the cheapest or have a winning personality.

It's never about how many hours you work – it's your output.

At some point you are going to have to swap your life for money, that's a fact of life. But if you can make it possible to be doing something you love, you're onto a winner.

Ian Crocker @Crockersaurus (called that because he's a dinosaur that doesn't tweet, hilarious, I know). He runs a company called Absolute Learning.

"Know your passions. What really excites you? What are you doing when time flies by? If you can make a living by doing what you love you'll never 'work' again.

Tell people how much you love doing what you do. Make sure every ounce of your enthusiasm is communicated, every time. People tell me that they're really enthusiastic about something – I ask them when their voice is going to find out!"

At times you'll have people telling you, with complete authority, that you've got it wrong.

Often well-meaning people. But they don't have your vision, your tenacity, your willingness to do what it takes to make a difference.

Everyone on your journey is meant to be there, but not everyone is meant to stay. Sometimes you have to give up on people, but you can never give up on yourself.

What you think is a setback often is a blessing in disguise. The most traumatic day in my life was set out in my second book, chapter 2, if you want to read it whilst "browsing" in Waterstones.

Have passion not only in your chosen business, but also in your decisions, by doing stuff you enjoy. As in really enjoy.

It was midnight on my 40th birthday and wifey was asleep next to me, and the business had been tough going the previous year or so. I remember lying there and thinking, what was I going to do for the next five years? Do I want to do this (4Networking) or not? BOOM, it came to me and I said to myself, yeah, I want to continue and finish the mission that I began in trying to make a positive difference.

But what HAS changed is, the truth is, I have no heart to make 4Networking international. Well, I don't, but perhaps I may find someone who will. But the idea of me sat in an airport lounge, doing what I'm doing now but internationally, makes no sense . . . to me. Anymore.

Remember I said that things change. Well, that also applies to your thinking.

What are you doing this for? In my case, changing the UK business scene forever is a big enough goal. But maybe your goal is simply all about changing your own life and your fortunes for the better. That's a good enough starting point.

Those without your passion may never understand your decisions.

@Aceofwaste, a self-made man who had a tough upbringing on the streets of Liverpool, owns a successful waste management company. He said, "You do something, you enjoy it to a certain degree, and as you get better at it you start to become more experienced and then that confidence translates into passion. But if in the early years you don't truly love what you do you're not gonna be able to grind yourself through the bollocks".

A job for life is no more – the only certainty is to try to give yourself the best chance of success. We are seeing the once gatekeepers of the high street falling away. Jessops. HMV. Game Station. Game. All have disappeared from my local high street in Taunton.

What has taken their place is a resurgence of those independent retailers who have decided that the difference between success and failure is not quitting.

The world is moving so fast.

The culture of my business was built by my design. I've driven it with a contagiously positive mindset which has spread through others to create a wave of change.

If you don't have culture by design, you have culture by default. Define your culture, what you stand for.

Always be busy, otherwise you end up being roped into doing stuff that isn't part of your plan. Busy may well be simply walking the dog, because the point I'm making is that if you leave your time open, someone else will fill it.

The passion thing can sound a bit trite, but I swear to you that being part of a business you truly love will ensure you beat every other business in the same profession whose sole reason for doing it is to make money.

Give people a reason to have an emotional connection with your business; they will help grow your passion and build your dream with you.

So what have you learned?

LIFE:

BUSINESS:

IDEAS:

Is your life/business likely to be that little bit easier? Y / N

5

THE DAY IT ALL CHANGED FOR YOU

There's a mate of mine who worked at Tesco's for about 12 years. He was involved in their management programme. The guy who trained my friend . . . let's call him Roger, had also been there for many years.

It was Roger's last day before retirement and one of the top brass, a director from HQ, was due to come down at 3pm and give him a proper send-off in front of all the staff.

2pm came and a call came in to the office.

"Hello Roger, it's (name withheld) from HQ here, how are you getting on?"

"Good, good."

". . . and how's the family?"

"Fine thanks."

"Erm Roger, what it is . . ."

When someone says Erm . . . your name, followed by "what it is . . ." you know what is coming is more often than not shit.

"You know that I was due to come down – well, we're opening a new store tomorrow and well, I've simply run out of time to get over to you today. So on behalf of myself and all the directors and indeed everyone within the company, I'd like to thank you for all your years of hard work. Really, thanks . . . again, sorry I couldn't make it and all the best for the future."

*click/

Roger relayed the conversation to my friend who is a wonderfully placid guy. Generally.

But instantly he filled with rage.

Fuming, absolutely fuming. How could they treat someone of such long-standing service in this manner? So he went against everything he'd ever been taught in his 12 years of Tesco management training and strode confidently onto the middle of the shop floor. This was his opportunity to right this injustice . . .

His Braveheart moment, to make a stand in front of the 100+ staff for his friend. He thought, even if none of the top brass could be arsed, he would give Roger the send-off he so rightly deserved.

You know what he did?

He stole a cake.

In all fairness it was reduced from £6 to £4 and smashed in on one side, a caterpillar cake, but don't worry he only needed four slices, as he, Roger and two other members of staff angrily tucked into the stolen booty.◤

Roger walked home that day, after 52 years of loyal service at Tesco's.

◤ Actually Officer, it may have been a petty cash purchase tbh, but never let the truth get in the way of the punchline of a good story!

No bottle of champagne.

No big send-off.

No exit interview.

Nothing, well unless you consider the stolen caterpillar cake.

FIFTY-TWO YEARS

FIFTY-TWO YEARS of weekends.

Think about that – FIFTY-TWO FRIGGIN' YEARS OF SERVICE and the director could not be arsed jumping in TO his, no doubt, top-of-the-range car for the three-hour drive for a man who had given his entire life to this organisation.

There would have been times in Roger's last 20 years when his children would have asked, "Dad, can we all go visit Alton Towers for the day or feed bread to the ducks at the pond at the weekend?" and he'd have said, "Sorry, I can't. You know weekends are our busiest time at the store and it pays really well so we can have nice **stuff**".

As we know, **every little helps . . .**

Imagine if I somehow managed to build a time machine and went back to visit Roger on his 40th birthday, materialised in front of him and showed him this book and let him read this chapter . . .

How would the direction of his life have changed? It might be that he would be delighted with how his last day of employment turned out. A boss that doesn't actually give two shits about him, his family or his 52 years of loyal servitude.

Think about the trajectory of your life right now . . .

On your last day of work. What are you on target for?

A caterpillar cake?

Or something more substantial? That's what this entire book is about.

Ensuring that the path you're currently on is the one you really want to be on.

Not a path that someone else has helpfully pointed you down.

The person who shared that story with me is a guy called Darren Clarke. He runs a cleaning company in the South West called @SpotlessSpaces.

Darren was that trainee. He was trained by Roger and the way he saw him treated that day changed everything.

The next day he handed in his notice.

One month later, he walked away. That was it. Finished. Over.

No more £60k salary, no healthcare plan, no company car. Nothing.

He swapped safe, secure and stable for fear, anxiety and a dream.

On his first day, wearing a £12 polo shirt with a clip art mop on it and a pocketful of *those* free business cards bearing his details, he went knocking on doors of houses offering his services. Some people laughed at him. One particular bloke answered the door, looked at his flyer and said, and I quote, "What's this shit?" before throwing his flyer on the floor in front of him.

Welcome to Darren's first day of self-employment. Lesser men would never have got to day two. Fast forward 18 months, he now employs 15 full-time staff.

This guy is such a hero of mine.

When he started his business, he had no guarantees, apart from one. A guarantee that he gave himself that he was not going to end up with a caterpillar cake.

Are you?

Sometimes people confuse bad decisions with bad luck. Your life and the direction it's taking is down to you.

Some say you have to live every day like it's your last. Cobblers. The problem in doing that is when you wake up tomorrow and you're still alive and you've blown all your mortgage money and ruined all your relationships.

What a great night though!

My take on this is that you have to **live every day *so it lasts***.

Denise McCallum, @DetectiveDenise – you'll find her quoted a few times in my second book.

She heard me speak at a big 4Networking meet and as a result took her life in a totally different direction. I didn't even know this until we bumped into each other at another meeting six months or so later, when she shared this with me.

She was arguably my biggest fan. ALWAYS had my back and worked with me on four or five occasions doing proper job detective work for me. Smart smart cookie, hyper perceptive about people and had an unassuming way of reading a situation faster than anyone I knew. She took in everything, whilst most would just see what most saw.

A couple of years back at a business conference, she told me that she had this slow burn cancer . . . "The doctors gave me two years to live, that was seven years ago," she laughed. "That's why I live and smile so much – it's no biggy about the cancer, after all we are all gonna go one day".

Denise did finally succumb to the cancer and I was asked to join three members of her family in carrying her coffin at her funeral. As I write this it all comes flooding back – first time I'd ever been asked to do this, what an honour. This was a lady I'd met through a networking event who read my book and credited me with changing the direction of her life.

At her wake the family released 99 red balloons, whilst the 80s song by Nina, *99 Red Balloons*, played. That was her song, the one that meant so much to her, the song that reminded her of the best of times, the time when she was a young girl and everything was so easy. Nice gesture time – listen to it next time you're on YouTube and then follow it by playing *your* song.

We all have one.

See, this is it, she changed the direction of her life, enjoying those last few years, taking the decisions she may have previously been uncertain about. These are the same decisions that you should be taking RIGHT NOW, instead of worrying about stuff which is just not worth worrying about.

Mark Bryant @MarkyMedia recalls our Denise – "I remember her getting drunk on several glasses of wine, and after having one too many she began munching on the flowers on the table, before carrying six drinks across a crowded pub (including a bottle of Corona in her cleavage!) without losing a drop, but then spilling them ALL over our table. She'd hot desk at my office and I was also with her when she experienced her first flight, from Newcastle to your Christmas party in Somerset!"

What would people say about you?

Are you the miserable sod that people avoid or are you full of life, zest and smiles?

That's what this is all about – I never knew when I started 4Networking the impact it would have across the UK. Of course I didn't.

But this is what seems to be my unwritten mission in life. To make a positive difference. It's always been my motivation. The more clout we each have, the more people we can each help.

Your mission. What is it?

At times we'll find ourselves having a whinge about life. About how things could be better, but think about this . . . how much of Steve Jobs' personal billions do you believe he would pay you to get just one more day of his life? I bet you wouldn't have to negotiate. He'd give you the lot, no arguments, and if the deal was done and he came back to Earth, do you reckon he'd spend that last day sat in front of an iMac, trying to work out the technical architecture of the new iPhone 7?

Of course not.

He'd be saying the things that really matter to him to the people that really matter to him.

It kinda puts things in perspective. If you are reading this, **you have something Steve Jobs and our Denise do not have.**

A tomorrow.

Stop reading for a second . . .

Think about that again.

You have a TOMORROW – sod that you have a TODAY.

Roy Hurley (Helder Engineering www.heldereng.com) was my original mentor and he talked to me about his transition to becoming self-employed: leaving a safe, secure job to start a business.

"It feels a scary, hard thing to do. Your friends, parents and peers will all advise against taking the risk. What if you fail? What if it doesn't work out? Well, if you really crash and burn and utterly fail in a complete way . . . then you will just have to get a job again. I mean, you have a job now, right? So you can get a job back if it all goes wrong.

So if you think about it, you are currently in the WORST POSSIBLE position you can be in, right now."

I know of a guy who worked all his life and died two weeks before he was due to retire on his generous pension.

Seriously.

Whilst there are others who live to be 100 and enjoy the *35 years* of pension and retirement.

Let's say you're going to live to be 100 – you work 65 of your best years of health

and wellness to then enjoy 35 of poor health in retirement. Really?

How about this for a radical idea. You *half* retire today and start going to the duck pond with your kids, start going to the gym, start living for today, not at the expense of tomorrow.

This is back to how I started this book. We've all been sold a pup, a big lie to keep us and our minds in stasis.

Grandad works all his life, putting away savings each and every month. He scrimps and saves, lives frugally so that when he passes on, all his accumulated wealth will be given to his grandchildren, who are so busy with their own lives that they never actually find the time to go and visit him.

But boy, there will be tears after he goes, as the recipients of his estate will fill the void left by their loss by buying 40" flat screen LED 3D 1080p televisions and having brand new fitted kitchens with custom cut granite work surfaces, in order to help with the grieving process you understand.

It doesn't make any sense.

So why do it?

When I'm at retirement age, I'm going to blow all my money on Caribbean cruises, full board mind. No Captain's buffet is going to be safe.

@Aceofwaste "I agree with not leaving the kids anything but for different reasons. Because it will rob them of something and cheat them from finding their own way. There is a value and confidence I have taken from what I have done, knowing that there was no safety net. I would never have got as far as I have if I'd thought there was a nice fat wedge to fall back on when my Mum and Dad pass away".

Sod the kids. As a parent, you've looked after them all their life – it'll be their turn to look after you.

Live YOUR life. Don't pass on any element of it, for someone else to enjoy.

Life. Business. Just got easier.

So what have you learned?

LIFE:

BUSINESS:

IDEAS:

Is your life/business likely to be that little bit easier? Y / N

6

WIN SOME.
LOSE NONE.

For so long when you start a business, it's just about survival. Living day to day. Paying the mortgage. Paying off the loan on the car.

You may feel like you are making no progress. But you are.

Even if the only thing you are progressing is your level of experience.

But experience doesn't pay the mortgage.

It does when you get enough of it. Your ability to make fast and correct decisions is sped up.

So instead of charging time for money, using an hourly rate, I charge for the job.

I'll give you an example. An office needs a computer fixing. Engineer #1 charges £60 an hour and takes three hours. £180.

Engineer #2 fixes it in 10 minutes and charges £110.

Some businesses would feel that the 10-minute solution is *bloody expensive* and would prefer an engineer to be sat in their office sipping their tea and tapping on a keyboard for three hours.

Sometimes people want to be blagged. It's ridiculous.

Sadly, the truth doesn't sell.

You might want to think about that when putting in your invoices. Ironically some would feel like they got more value for money from Engineer #1.

People would overlook the fact that the reason Engineer #2 can do the job in 10 minutes, when other techs would take three hours, is because of the experience gained over many years. The first time *they* encountered this problem, it *also* took them a few hours, but they invested that time many years ago.

I launched www.BradCamp.Biz. It's my vehicle to be as outrageous and honest about business as I like and in essence really spread to individuals and businesses the kind of teachings which you find within my books.

At each BradCamp I wheel out a special guest to support me. People like @RachelElnaugh, the first female Dragon in series 1 and 2 of *Dragon's Den*. I round up experts, not only peeps with business experience, but more importantly, with those business scars, the likes of which you get when things don't go the way you expect.

Anyway, the first one was held over in Bradford and I remember driving up there with @debbiehuxton, my coach (more about her later) and wingman for that BradCamp and we were both gripped by fear.

As in petrified. I've been doing this sort of stuff for 8+ years, but then for no logical reason your mind starts playing tricks on you, trying to cheat you into failure.

Next day, the event was just awesome. The anxiety during the previous night's drive was unfounded. The event was life and direction changing for the 20+ attendees.

The run-up to the second event was faultless, with everything organised perfectly.

Then it all went wrong. The venue was due to be open at 7:00 for an 8:30 start.

Quarter to nine and still the venue hadn't opened.

When the manager of the chosen venue finally rolled out of bed, I didn't have time to listen to his excuses, as I had a room to organise. Not to worry, as I had 15 or so delegates who had been waiting out in the cold for 40 minutes to help me move tables.

Can you imagine?

Awful. Just awful. Throughout the entire session, I just couldn't get into a proper flow. Jangled by someone else's mistakes.

You are going to get times in your life when the cards you are dealt are not what you would have wanted. But you have to play on.

The best learnings you will get in life are from losing.

Think back to one of those times when you lost. When things didn't go your way, you got a bucketful of life experience.

That's how it is sometimes – you have to deal with what you have in front of you. This is what makes great business people. Those that don't allow themselves to be bounced into a quitting mentality.

Tough experiences have taught me so much and being battle hardened in your field will allow you to do amazing things.

I described that second BradCamp as a narrow points victory. A "W" in the Win, Lose, Draw column is a win, no matter how slim.

Whilst sticking with the boxing metaphors, don't lose the fight before you've thrown the first punch. Even when you are strongest, you can be weak.

See, that's what makes people, like say pro boxers, stay at the top of their game – it's not only their ability to throw and take punches in a gym, but the whole package.

There are numerous examples of amazing athletes that just can't cope with it when the curtains roll back.

I was dicking about on Twitter, and came across this heavyweight boxer called Derek Chisora, he fought former world champion David Haye.

Anyways, some tw@t starts ripping into Derek:

"You're a bum, a rubbish boxer, etc."

He then said this classic, "I wouldn't mind getting knocked out for £3,000,000!"

I tweeted him back, "Why don't you then?"

"What?" he responded.

"Why don't you go get in the ring and get KO'd for 3 million quid?"

What followed were about 15 tweets from me . . . I was on one.

I'll tell you why, because of the preceding 15 years of getting up at 4am each weekday morning, running the cold, wet streets of East London, no crowds, no adulation. Just cold mornings, weekends, whilst his friends were out clubbing, drinking pints of lager and eating KFC, he'd have to abstain. Staying in, drinking pints of raw eggs, watching what he ate. Then at weekends getting 100s of heavy medicine balls to the stomach, in between the 500 sit ups and four hours of gym time, everything an up-and-coming boxer has to do along with rounds and rounds of amateur fights, where the best reward you can wish for is a W in the Win, Lose, Draw column.

And then, then after 15 or so years of living like that . . .

You may *get lucky* and "win" the chance to earn a few million whilst the world's media tunes in to watch you running the risk of getting violently knocked out in a brutal fashion by someone who has trained equally hard for the previous 15 years in the art of throwing punches.

People like this idiot on Twitter don't want to do the 15 years of hard graft needed to get the experience to cut it at the highest level. They think you just want to wear a spangly boxer's robe with your name embroidered on the shoulders, step into the ring and luck out and walk away with a big cheque.

Life isn't like that. Get your head around it. Luck is what you create for yourself.

I've spoken at over 1,000 events since I began my own business and at one of these, @DougieBrimson was in the audience. I didn't know it at the time, but he wrote the screenplay for the Hollywood film *Green Street* which starred Elijah Wood.

Sorry, my bad, Prince Charles told me not to name drop. Anyways, Dougie saw me speak and was so blown away that he introduced me to the top man at a TV production company, you'd have heard of them.

I got invited to an initial meeting, where we just hit it off, and it was hinted that I could head up my own TV show on a main terrestrial channel.

WOW . . . just amazing, I could already envisage me having my own TV show . . .

That first meeting was just awesome. I seeped brilliance, confidence, intelligence, charisma and razor sharp wit and humour. The guy said I had it all, the whole package.

I told those around me about the meeting and was already seeing myself in the Sundays falling out of China White's with the girls from *TOWIE* . . .

As I drove home, I excitedly called my Mum and told her, "All I need to do now is to impress the remainder of his team, the hard bit's been done!"

A few days later I got the call, the invite back in, and headed in with fresh new trainers, new T-shirt. I was going to be the best I could possibly be.

There I was, waiting in reception for this second meeting with the top man I'd met and the rest of his team. The heat started to build up within me, the enormity of this situation started to grow, as my mind raced over and over . . . my initial confidence tipped over into fear.

The sweat began pouring off my face. This was a cool October day, not the height of summer.

I went into the room and I was already burning up. One of the team said, "It is a bit hot in here", but it wasn't.

They asked me to tell me a bit about myself. Ha, normally my favourite subject and ordinarily this situation is a walk in the park and I'd do my thing. But here I just began motor mouthing, blabbering absolute cod shit . . . just rubbish.

The sweat by this time was visible to all at the meeting. If I'd been sat on their side of the table, I'd have been thinking this guy is on drugs. Which frazzled my thinking even more, as I knew what they would be thinking, and so I got even more flustered.

The one thing I was doing really well though was fretting.

At the end of the 20-minute meeting, they said they'd go away and have an internal meeting and come back to me . . .

They never did.

This wasn't my time, I wasn't ready for my own TV show. But next time I get an opportunity like it, I'll be so much better and less likely to unravel because of the experience I gained through losing!

I've since been contacted by the production team behind Channel 4's *The Secret Millionaire*. The premise of the show, as I'm sure you know, is that a rags-to-riches successful UK business person, goes back to their town of birth with a camera team and pretends to be looking for work.

I said to the wife, how good would that be? Going around the streets of Salford, pretending my name is John, a welder and this is a programme on long-term unemployment.

She said you don't need a camera crew following you to make a difference.

She had a point.

But I can imagine what it would have been like. On that first day going to Salford boys boxing club, where a little copper-haired eight-year-old lad, Tommy, jabs at the bag, full of enthusiasm, with me stood behind the bag, as he rat-a-tat-tats it.

I know your Dad's banged up mate, but you stay away from the gangs and the drugs Tommy, you got a future in this game . . .

And that evening, back in my bedsit, sobbing uncontrollably (whilst a full camera crew films me/raises eyebrow) about how much Tommy reminds me of me as a kid . . .

. . . without the *ginger hair*.

And the next day, me heading over to Ethel's soup kitchen. Ethel has been there for over 20 years helping the homeless people of Manchester:

"Why do you do it Ethel?"

"I'jus like 'elpin the lost generation, *oh and I need a new cooker*".

And on the final day of filming, *The Secret Millionaire* BIG reveal. I'd turn up outside Ethel's soup kitchen in my Rolls Royce Phantom, number plate BB1. My chauffeur would step out and open my door. I adjust my three-piece suit and pocket watch and confidently stride towards the door. Ethel looks up from her beef broth, "J-Jo-John what are you doing here?"

"Ethel, you may want to take a seat, as I have TWO secrets to share with you today –

The first secret is that my name is NOT John. It is in fact Brad Burton and I'm a dynamic entrepreneur from around the UK and the second secret Ethel," reaching into my

Life. Business. Just got easier.

inside pocket, "the second secret", grabbing my cheque book and Mont Blanc pen, "the second secret is, I'm NOT a millionaire and these cheques are gonna friggin' bounce!"

I just made myself LOL with that story.

It IS absolutely true about them approaching me, twice now. It's also absolutely true that I'm not a millionaire and funnily enough, I'm nowhere as driven as I once was about ever being one.

Things change.

But as a result of the business decisions I've made, I think it's fair to say I am in the best position that I've ever been in my life.

The six-month lease came up for the rented house we were staying in after selling our two-up two-down. And so it was time we looked for a place to buy. I left it with the wife, as I concentrated on the business. She told me, aside from needing proximity to the children's school, that ever since being a kid she wanted a house with a wood burner.

What the F is a wood burner?

Honestly, coming from Salford, Manchester, the idea that you light a fire inside your house and don't run for insurance purposes made no sense to me.

If you've ever tried to light a wood burner, you'll need matches, firelighters, and what you don't do is try to burn big logs first. You have to get kindling going and work your way up, otherwise you'll just extinguish your flame.

It is exactly the same principle with your business. I know you want the good stuff. But if you try to get it too fast, you put yourself in danger of smothering everything you have worked for.

As long as each day you are making small incremental gains, that's OK. Beware the certainty sales people who offer you big gains fast.

Nine years in business, I am yet to encounter a genuine big gain, fast. Not one.

I've spent hundreds of thousands of £££ in the last nine years on biz stuff, and I can say with 100% certainty there are no "services" that will turn your fortunes around instantly . . . no matter how expensive, no matter how cheap an option.

There are **no shortcuts** – instead, look to get little teeny incremental gains . . . lots and lots of times.

All I have ever wanted to do in my books is share the things that other books on biz don't. The reality. The fear. You are human. You are normal.

It's OK to be shit scared because one day that fear turns to courage.

The right choice is often not the easy one. You'll never grow a business without taking risks, and there are times when you will lose. But remember you always win.

@Crockersaurus "One simple step is to remove the phrase 'if only' from our vocabulary and replace it with 'next time'. If you ever hear yourself (or indeed anyone else) using 'if only' then confront it. Too late! It's gone! We can only work with 'next time', learning from our experience and making positive changes going forward".

Finally another mainstream TV opportunity happened. BBC2's *Newsnight* wanted me to go on at short notice and talk about the impact of EU-imposed regulation on small business.

Ha, as you can imagine this is a subject I know loads about (not)! But by the time I'd driven the 40 minutes to the studio, I'd spoken to some carefully chosen people who DID know, who briefed me with enough to get by. As they say, it's not what you know, it's who you know, and with experience, that's all you need.

See me on *Newsnight* here (http://BradBurton.Biz)

Win some. Lose none. Don't be discouraged.

Throw enough balls at a coconut and you will eventually win a goldfish.

But it does help if you've got big balls.

So what have you learned?

LIFE:

BUSINESS:

IDEAS:

Is your life/business likely to be that little bit easier? Y / N

Life. Business. Just got easier.

7

EJECT. EJECT. EJECT.

I want you to let your imagination kick in for a minute. Think about a plane on an airfield. It's a fighter plane. The pilot walks up in his RAF flight suit and reaching the bottom of the ladder he begins to climb up. Sat in the cockpit, he starts doing the appropriate checks.

AVIONICS	**OK**
FUEL/OIL	**OK**
ENGINE	**OK**
UNDERCARRIAGE	**OK**
FLAPS	**OK**

Go ahead from the tower. "Zero One Niner, you are clear for take off . . ."

Taxiing and then taking off to reach an altitude of 10,000 ft, the pilot pushes the lever forward, firing up the afterburners, the acceleration pushing him into the back of his seat.

Then an almighty and sudden bang causes the plane to shudder violently and a malfunction notification appears on the heads-up display, as the automated voice bellows

*"WARNING / **WARNING** / ENGINE FAILURE / EJECT EJECT **EJECT**"*

If you or I were sitting in the pilot seat, we'd be bending forward, instinctively looking for the ejection seat arming handle . . .

Not a fighter pilot. These guys have trained for seven years for this. They've read books on the physics of flying, on dealing with emergencies. They've logged endless hours of simulator time learning to deal with this kind of situation.

But now, this is not a computer simulation. This is the real deal.

```
8,000 ft
7,000 ft
6,000 ft
WARNING / WARNING / ENGINE FAILURE /
EJECT EJECT EJECT
Is this recoverable?
Keep reading the dials
Work out what is going on
Get as much information as to why

3,000 ft
WARNING / WARNING / ENGINE FAILURE /
EJECT EJECT EJECT
This situation has happened

2,000 ft
8 seconds till impact, that's practically
a lifetime in a fighter pilot's world.
1,000 ft
900 ft
WARNING / WARNING / ENGINE FAILURE /
EJECT EJECT EJECT
800 ft
700 ft
```

Life. Business. Just got easier.

A fighter pilot's priority is to save the plane.

Only at the last possible moment would they even *consider* ejecting!

Welcome to SELF-EMPLOYMENT/YOUR JOB/YOUR LIFE (Delete as applicable)

You are flying a plane that you, yes YOU, designed. For years you've played it out in your head as to what your life would be. Now this is real.

In your mind's eye your plane was this bad-ass, sleek, matt black stealth war machine, and then as it taxis along the runway and struggles into the air, it's like something out of a frigging Charlie Chaplin film. Barely able to maintain or gain altitude, all too quickly losing altitude.

We spend too much time focusing on the stuff like the matt black paint, as that's easy to apply and made it look really impressive.

We avoid doing the really difficult stuff like avionics and control systems.

Then we as pilots of our planes have *shocked face* when flying it is so difficult.

Some blame the government or the economic climate for their failing businesses, whilst others use this "downturn" to gain height.

I meet people blaming their upbringing for their woes in later life. I have met others who have used that shit from childhood or background to make a positive difference.

It's OK for you though Brad . . .

You know, it's at least 10 times now since I started out in business over nine years ago where I have wanted to quit and pull the ejection handle.

If 1 is not quitting and 10 is quitting. I've been 9.8, 9.9 at least 10 times.

Many times I've had well-meaning people suggesting I eject and "go get a proper job" – at least you know where you stand, with a proper job!

Tell that to staff at Comet, Woolworths, Game.

Do you know the real reason why I didn't pull the ejection handle on each of those occasions?

The truth is, I didn't have a friggin' ejection handle.

Mentally, I'd got rid of it.

I just didn't have the option to quit. Instead, there has always been and will always be the option to adapt.

I'm still here. Why? Because I didn't have a Plan B.

If you have a Plan B, you'll never make your Plan A work.

Why? Because you don't 100% believe in your Plan A.

Otherwise you wouldn't have a Plan B.

How seriously do you take a business owner punting a product/service that they don't 100% believe in?

You can often sense it a mile away, that lack of belief, and straightaway all credibility is blown.

As a result, they don't sell whatever product/service Plan A is and start looking towards Plan B as their saviour.

But Plan B is doomed from the start, as it is backed by even less belief than Plan A!

How the hell can you expect people to believe in you if you don't believe in yourself?

By all means have a flexible Plan A but it has to be a Plan A.

I have met Independent Financial Advisers (IFAs), who have been in the game for 20+ years moving away from their profession in order to pursue a *Ground Floor Opportunity*, to sell the latest Multi-Level Marketing thing. At networking events they now "wear several hats".

If only people would stick to the one thing they are good at instead of being seduced by the bling of every seemingly quick cash opportunity.

For those IFAs that are daft enough to stay in the IFA game, is there more or less business for them? More, of course. Often the difference between success and failure is not quitting.

The world has changed. Business doesn't just fall out of trees like perhaps it once did, so you now need to be more inventive in winning business. Start with this – how are you fundamentally different from your nearest competitor?

- We offer a free one-hour review.
- We speak plain English, a language the client can understand.
- We really get to know the client.

So do your competitors.

There is generally a long way to go from the minute a **red warning** light comes on in a situation. But most "normal" people panic, lose their heads, at the very point when you can recover your plane. Let's move away from that metaphor now.

If you lose hope, you lose the fight. Sometimes all you will have in a situation is *misplaced* hope, but it will carry you just that little further on until you find your answer.

The difference between winning and losing is not giving up. So many times you'll question your own logic.

It took me 32 years to find my path. Do the right thing and **stop blaming the Eurozone, Clegg Cameron, interest rates, horse meat, anything . . . for your problems.**

When playing with a dead man's hand, only you know when you should fold or go all in. Yet I see so many people who just run out of gas, having spent time on folly. A business just doesn't stop working overnight, so you have to be smart enough to move with market changes. Again, the same principle I have been talking about throughout this book, little and often.

I'm not a footy fan. I don't really get it, but I did watch the highlights of a Man United game, where they came back from 3–0 down at half time to win 5–3 against Tottenham.

You don't have to understand the beautiful game to see the lessons. That is a champion's mind, the ability to know that until that final whistle is blown, a situation can still be turned around.

They never give up.

Playing the game *Words* with friends on the iPad (think of it a bit like an online *Scrabble*) I'm steaming ahead, got a nice 30-point lead, midway through the game. When my opponent @Just_Dee_X does an uber triple word score word for a 99 pointer. My morale fell away instantly. The previous confidence changed in an instant as the tiles were placed. I felt it was an impossible game to turn round. Whether it was or it wasn't, in my mind I felt I'd already lost.

With my confidence gone, the best I could hope for was adding an "S" tile to ZOO.

Life can be like that. One moment you're 30 points up, the next 70 down. But unlike *Words* with friends, you shouldn't just press the *Forfeit Game* button, you have to keep going.Any time you find yourself in a difficult situation, ask yourself, "What do I have to do to turn this situation around?" And then go do it.

I know it's tough, but you can do this. Really you can. Give yourself a talking too, lock that belief down. Lock that belief in.

At times you'll feel like a human version of the board game *Buckaroo*, but you can carry a whole load of miner's pickaxes and ropes, more than you think, before you have to buck off.

I have a photo of the moment when the shit hit the fan in my business life, and at that point, I didn't know if I could carry on. That's the truth and @4NTerryCooper our Chairman and Co-Director @NoRedBraces were there for me.

When you are at your weakest, most vulnerable, that's the time when you too will see who is really there for you, when you find out who chooses to step up and stand shoulder to shoulder with you, even if they are as fearful as you may feel.

They don't show it.

Now and again, if things are not going your way, you may find yourself on the receiving end of *the curse of the self-employed*, being tempted to have a shufty through the job section of Thursday's paper, but you are mentally putting yourself back.

Don't waste time looking for a job, look for a client.

If, however, it's REALLY not worked out for you, you've tried, given it your all there is just no point in going down with the metaphorical plane. By all means go back to get a proper job, but at least you are now armed with the knowledge that *you know where you stand*.

A friend of mine @grahampsmith ran his own accountancy practice. He held on for about four years but it just didn't work out.

He's now back in a *proper* part-time job and at some point in the future he may try to start his own business again.

I asked him why it didn't work out . . .

"I stopped focusing on my core business, having pissed away loads of money trying hyper ambitious website stuff that even if it worked probably couldn't have *really* worked.

We weren't geared up or ready for customers, and we listened too much to marketers who spent six months "researching" the feasibility of our new web-based accountancy online magic.

The difference was that they quite liked the meter running. I didn't.

I became disillusioned with that, and then when the opportunity came along to invest, open and help to run a boutique coffee shop in my home town, I jumped at it. Even saying *boutique coffee shop* now makes me cringe".

This was never going to end well.

"I ploughed about £30k into it for my share of the business set up. We then spent too much of that time and money sitting in the solicitor's office, talking about risk mitigation, exit strategies and drafting shareholders' agreements. We effectively, as you say Brad, had a three-way *dicking about* session, with the small problem that this was at £500 an hour even before our time was taken into account.

That's a lot of lattes you have to sell.

During one of these sessions, I actually said, 'The thing that is going to kill this business is something we've missed and are not discussing in this room'".

Grand Opening.

The customers came in and the coffee flowed out.

Then a few days later, the land opposite, where our customers would park, had the gate pulled closed and a big padlock added to it. Our landlord was in a dispute with *another* landlord about the parking but failed to mention this when we signed the lease.

Two months later – **Grand Closing**.

> We could have taken it to court, but the only one who would have won would have been the solicitors."

I ask Graham at what point did he as a mild-mannered accountant think that he could be the next Theo Paphitis?

> "I thought I had the skills needed in this area and the romantic vision of being an investor took over."

The curse of *Dragon's Den* strikes again, as everyone thinks they can be an investor, just as everyone who has ever watched Kirstie & Phil thinks they can create a buy-to-let portfolio and make £50k a pop.

Only invest what you are prepared to lose.

If you're not 100% committed, don't do it.

Concentrate on what you are good at! An accountant whose only experience of coffee is ordering one had the odds stacked against him.

But it may well have panned out OK if it wasn't for those *Scooby Doo* style pesky landlords!

Back to Graham, he tells me that by him doing the part-time thing, what he's finding is that the pressure to perform has fallen away, and because he's no longer desperate to sell his services, he's finding that his services are selling themselves . . .

Life. Business. Just got easier.

I've said it before, *desperate sweaty salesmen sell nothing*. Ever.

Remember, it was my all-too-evident sweat that gave me away in that TV production meeting.

Stop chasing every great idea, settle on one and make it happen!

EJECT. EJECT. EJECT.

IGNORE. IGNORE. IGNORE.

So what have you learned?

LIFE:

BUSINESS:

IDEAS:

Is your life/business likely to be that little bit easier? Y / N

Life. Business. Just got easier.

8
JENGA!

You'll have times in your life when things don't go your way and times when they do.

There comes a point when everyone reaches breaking point. I'm going to share mine.

That day was back in early 2011. My business was on the final day of our Welcome Back campaign, which turned out to be our best day ever, turning over 50% <u>more</u> in one day than we did in the entire first year of the company back in 2006.

A cause for celebration I think you'll agree.

Well it would have been if my marriage wasn't about to end.

See, at the time of writing, as those who have read my previous books will know, I've actively been on the road for the last six years, doing up to 1,000 miles each week at speaking gigs, interviews, 4Networking meetings, it's been relentless.

Away four nights a week, me and the now "not so supportive" wife had just grown apart. Well that's not strictly true, but we'd begun to take each other for granted, we just weren't really interested in each other anymore.

After 15 years of being together, maybe that's what happens with all long-term relationships.

Prior to this, a little known fact, I'd been sleeping on a moody beat-up old leather sofa for years at our previous two-bed house in the early days of 4Networking, as the wife said I snored and kept her awake – she even showed me video footage that she took and yup, it's true I did.

Then when I moved into our current place, we continued that habit and I had my own bedroom and wife had hers.

I'd get home after five days on the road and she wouldn't even look up from her iPad.

"She doesn't understand me."

"We are more flatmates than husband and wife."

The night of the 4Networking Christmas Do, the wife chose not to come, opting for an evening at a pantomime with the kids, arranged on the same night.

This as a result left the door open for someone else to walk through it. Or it could have . . .

That's not what happened.

But it could have. Sometimes even when the sign on the border of a field says BEWARE MINEFIELD, we still enter knowing that.

A couple of months later, an appointment was scheduled with a divorce solicitor.

The marriage was over. It wasn't really going anywhere.

Or maybe it wasn't just the marriage. It was the stress from everything else that was massively compounding it all.

I was kept in a sustained and constant level of high stress and it was taking its toll on my wellbeing.

During this time, I confided in my good friend of many years, @MarkyMedia about how I was feeling, and he said, your life is like a game of *Jenga*.

Do you know the game *Jenga*? Fifty-four individual wooden bricks, built into a tower. The player takes a brick from the bottom of a tower and places it on top. As the game goes on the tension builds as the height rises and the integrity of the structure begins to wobble. With every move it becomes more likely that the tower will collapse in on itself.

I met a life coach type woman at one of my networking groups and we had a 10 minute 1–2–1.

She said, "Can I be really honest with you?"

"Of course."

"You are suffering from anxiety and high levels of stress."

I feigned a laugh. "What makes you say that?"

"Seven years as an A&E nurse with a specialism in stress management within the NHS."

"OK, OK, let's talk."

Enter @debbiehuxton. Not that I felt she could help me. After all, as everyone knows, I quite like a bit of stress, it fires me up. But this was all too much.

I arranged to meet her after the meeting.

She asked me this question, "Are you willing to risk it all?"

The thing about coaches is that they say very little and whilst that's not strictly the case when I coach people, proper ones who have qualifications and that sort of stuff, do.

I broke down crying.

In typical Brad style, I asked Debbie what was happening and was told I was having a "nervous breakdown" which is a polite/posh way of saying, you are temporarily mental.

Combine this relationship breakdown with heading up a company that had lost its way – two directors had moved on six months or so prior. And add in a load of unnecessary employment bullshit to deal with too. Then relentless fallout relating to changes, twinned with this mental minefield I'd got myself into.

If I was Mariah Carey, I'd likely have cancelled my future tour dates, citing "exhaustion" but I wasn't, so I had to continue running the business.

When you pull the pin out in your life, make sure you know which way you are throwing the grenade.

The whole week had been like an episode of *24*, with the situation unfolding and changing minute by minute. Right at the height of business success, I was at my lowest in recent years, crying uncontrollably, unable to use that laser beam decision-making ability which had become my trademark. I was ill.

I'm fixed now.

twitch

If you can see the warning signs, you too can avoid burnout. Mark Smith is a hypnotherapist who has also carved out a 20-year career as a professional drummer.

I was lucky enough to see him in action – he runs an amazing workshop called @Drumnosis, uses both hypnosis AND drumming to make a point, both LOUD and clear.

I grabbed him for a chat after the session.

Do you think you can multi-task, he asked.

Of course fella, I'm king of it.

"No, you are not Brad. Multi-tasking is myth. What people do is lots of individual tasks, one thing at a time."

He then demonstrated that with a simple 1,2,1,2 beat on his drum kit, gradually speeding it up to the point where it sounded like he was doing two things at once, even though it wasn't.

He then did a more complicated combination of drum beats, before telling me to do the beats I did with my right hand with my left and vice versa.

Easy at first, then as he sped up the beats, I was all over the shop.

"When people take on too much or do stuff that they are not experienced in, things start misfiring, and before you know it, the anxiety builds, because you are making bad beats. This creates more anxiety, as you think more about the mistake you just made, and the subconscious then begins to make more and more mistakes.

Depending on the situation, this creates an outcome such as depression or feelings of being uncomfortable in everyday situations. Or, in your case Brad, a breakdown.

(Continued)

You were handling too many things, in areas that you don't know how to deal with.

When you become stressed the brain tells the nervous system to release adrenaline and cortisone and this creates many different effects – the body has a physical response, expressed through the nervous system.

Think of it like how you feel when you first started public speaking –

- Heart rate speeds up
- Blood vessels shrink (this is what can cause heart attacks)
- Lungs widen
- Increased rate of breathing
- Digestive system shuts down, hence "butterflies" in the stomach or feeling sick.

We've likely all experienced situations that make us feel that way.

When you're in that mode for an extended time, other additional problems arise, things which affect our behavioural systems – constant agitation, insomnia, a what's-the-point, I-can't-be-arsed-to-get-out-of-bed mindset and an inability to concentrate as our body and mind shuts down to try to escape from this often seemingly impossible situation.

In extreme stress, you may also get visual problems arising from muscles of strained eyes.

All these signs are your alarm system. You can't stay in that situation."

It's a bit like when a computer suddenly crashes or a system shuts down. We can all deal with a certain level of anxiety, but if that level is overloaded, that's when those blue screens of death happen, but in your life.

It's a bit like a checkout at a supermarket – no matter how fast you do it, you can only scan one thing at a time.

Debbie said to me, "Forever is a long time, are you serious about divorcing?"

I said, "Yes", and she said, "Do you trust me?" "Of course." "Right, I want you to do one thing." "What's that?"

"Don't make a decision today. Wait a week. Let's get your thinking clearer. Right now you can't make a balanced or informed decision."

She was right.

So, under her advice, instead of munching valium each evening at bedtime, I started listening to frigging whale songs in order to sleep at night.

Each time we cheat, be it sleeping tablets to catch up on sleep, or any shortcut in life, we are masking the real issue. Short term that kind of works, but long term it never works.

Never make a long-term decision on a short-term emotion.

The underlying lesson in all this is to make sure on your quest for success, you **don't put at risk the very thing that you are currently sacrificing it all for.**

Right now you have three areas that are important to you in your life –

HEALTH / WEALTH / REALTH

Realth, you may have heard it – it stands for relationships (and it also rhymes).

Mark each of these on a score of 1–10 (1 bad/10 good)

HEALTH [ ]
WEALTH [ ]
REALTH [ ]

If you are being really honest, you're likely to admit that one of 'em is way out. The one that is all out of kilter, which if you don't at the very least acknowledge is out of step, is likely to create problems that spill out and impact on the other two.

It may be easier think of it as a sliding scale

Left 3	2	1	2	Right 3
HEALTH				**WEALTH**
REALTH				

If you had to circle a number where you are at this point in time, where would you be?

Maybe there is a way of getting it smack bang in the middle, but I think you have to dip heavily into the H/R side. In my case I had to do this at least for the first few years or so in order to finally get the right balance.

In my experience, in the first few years of running a business, everything pays the price – poor health, poor realth and no wealth.

It really helps to be aware that is likely to be the case. Because it's all too easy to get demoralised thinking you are some kind of failure.

Life. Business. Just got easier.

That's just how it is.

Now six years on, I should have been through all that, but I wasn't and I nearly paid a high price. But true strength is holding it all together when everyone expects you to fall apart, which is what I did. Getting this "campaign" to market, and literally on our best day ever, I crashed and burnt.

Quite heroic/stupid [delete as applicable].

Are you currently building a big tall *Jenga* tower which your peers admire and talk about, one that you feel proud of, at the expense of stability in your life?

That thing, you know THAT thing, address it today before it causes YOUR *Jenga* tower to collapse.

I don't know what tomorrow brings, but I do know this – you can't run from your head. Have a think about what your core values are, what it is that drives you, and why are you living the life and walking the path you now talking about.

Returning to that Health, Wealth, Realth.

I do hope the one that has the lowest score is for wealth. It's the least important of the three.

Don't get me wrong, we would all prefer to have more money rather than less. But is having more wealth at the expense of health or realth on the sliding scale worth it?

Nervous breakdowns
Family/relationship breakdowns

Is that what you really want?

Everything is valuable in two situations. Firstly, when getting it, secondly when losing it.

Understand this, nothing lasts forever. Not even your problems.

All problems have a worst-before date.

Throughout this difficult time, Debbie helped keep me from unravelling, with almost tunnel vision, taking time out to give me a call throughout all the periods where I walked the dog and on one of my calls Debbie asked me the same question she opened with –

"Are you willing to risk it all?"

"What do you mean by all?"

"Just answer the question", she said firmly.

"Are you willing to risk it all?"

Ask yourself that same question.

So now you are aware of the pitfalls of the pursuit of success, with that in mind, you'll be better placed to avoid them.

That whole period of my life, I wouldn't change. If sharing it with you the reader, helps just one person through a tough time, then it's been worth it.

Things get worse before they get better, but when they do, remember throughout your difficult and testing times, those who picked you up and those that tried pushing you down.

One thing and one thing alone will determine your fate – your mind.

Keep it clean.

The most important decisions in life aren't easy.

The company has finally turned this latest corner, with time moving the whole situation into the filing cabinet marked *Past*.

We never did get divorced and things are on the mend.

We lose so many todays worrying about how life may be tomorrow.

That sounds like a chapter heading to me . . .

To avoid a war, sometimes all you need to do is plot a course for your aircraft carrier.

So what have you learned?

LIFE:

BUSINESS:

IDEAS:

Is your life/business likely to be that little bit easier? Y / N

9

BUY MY STUFF/ NEVER TRUST A SKINT TELEMARKETER

Never trust a skint telemarketer. If they're that good at what they do, why the hell are they skint? Same goes for telemarketers who offer their services via an email.

The best cold callers I've ever met are either drug addicts, alcoholics or mental.

The most effective one I ever had the good fortune to work with, way back, was all three. He also was skint, because he spent all his money on drugs and alcohol to help deal with his issues.

So maybe there's the exception to the rule.

Surely the best way to show how great you are is by demonstrating it in your manner on the telephone or your skill in bypassing a PA. There was this one time I shared a car journey with an IFA who was courting me for my business and he was doing quite a good job. However, the SERVICE DUE (–5473 miles) warning light which kept flashing up like a frigging Christmas tree light on his dashboard was at odds with his assertion that he was the best in the market for wealth generation. It was one of those social conditions where we both pretended not to see it *every time* it blinked.

It was not the greatest of starts on the road to instilling me with confidence in him. What sort of silent messages are you sending about your business? Are you supremely confident about it? If not, why not? What's got to change in order to fix it to get you supremely confident?

I've just come back from my second and final session at the dentist for a root canal.

Honestly, when I got the emergency appointment a few weeks back and I was hit with the £400 price tag, **I grimaced and thought, "You robbing bastard!"**

If it wasn't for the pain of the abscess when I sought out the dentist, I would have walked away right then. I'd have been gone.

It's the equivalent of the modern day highwayman. At least he had the decency to wear a mask throughout the entire procedure.

Now the pain has gone and the work has been done, my point of view has changed.

I no longer feel I've been robbed, but actually believe I've received amazing value for money.

Let me explain.

- Four hours in total.
- Two-person team.
- Years of studying to be qualified to do it.
- Thousands of pounds' worth of specialist equipment.
- Comfortable, well-maintained premises.
- Receptionist.
- Support team IT holding it all together.
- Insurance.
- Business rates.

Taking that little lot into account, I have to say the £400 price tag was an absolute bargain.

Thank you, Mr Dentist of Weston-super-Mare.

Fear not Brad fans, this is not my column submission for *Dentist Monthly*. I want you to transfer my initial reaction of "£400 you robbing bastard" into the context of your own business.

There are times in life when being "expensive" should be seen as reassurance.

We've all submitted a quote or a meticulously put-together proposal, only to find that the first thing the potential buyer does when it lands in their inbox is bypass the first five pages you spent two days on and whizzes straight to the last page, you know, the bit on the bottom right, where it lists your price.

This proposal will then be used as a weapon to beat you up or even worse used to shave down your competitors' quotes – "John, beat this and it's yours".

On that basis, I stopped doing heavyweight proposals a long time ago. Buyers seem to only be interested in the price, not how you came to that conclusion. As long as you've sold in the value at the front end, there's less need for an in-depth document. That's old-school thinking right there.

Since taking my no-nonsense, back-of-fag-packet approach to proposals with both my consultancy and my speaking jobs, I've never lost a gig yet – the sale is done in the first few minutes, not the last few.

You'll find on the path to being a genius, you'll first pass through several stops at the stations marked "You're mad".

It's a brave new world – one of teeny proposals – but it works. Beautifully, in my world.

Next time you're asked for a proposal to progress an opportunity, think about the path that's been taken and the experience that allows someone to bottom line you with a price point that, after the event, can only be described as great value and not that of a robbing bastard.

It was after one of my networking events in Glasgow, I had a dinner meeting scheduled. One of the ladies recommended a lovely place called Oasis restaurant where they do wonderful tapas, just perfect, you can never have too many salted potatoes.

2.8 miles later, the satnav chirped that I had arrived at my destination.

In my mind's eye, and based on the testimony of my referee, I'd anticipated some basil and rock salt potatoes, with chrome designer tables, pot plants and a fancy atrium.

Turning the corner I arrived at the 'asis restaurant, navigated the car park potholes and waited for the second car to arrive.

The chef smoking out the back must be used to seeing this happen – the other car pulled up alongside and we feigned some conversation and ended up diving away to a national chain nearby.

That YES, No, Maybe decision making is being done every day in so many situations and more and more we are living by that code.

Two cars of people arrived and left without spending a penny. With the money they'd earned from our visit, they could likely have invested in the acrylic O that was missing from the sign. Faulty restaurant signage – if you can't get that right, what's the food gonna be like?

What is your "shop front" saying about you? Be it in business or in life, everything from your business card, demeanour, the way you speak and attitude to things.

In the second restaurant, they assertively yet beautifully handled us. Putting dessert menus into our hands. None of this, "Would sir like to see the dessert menu?" nonsense.

Multiply that by as many people who sit down in that place. That's a small fortune each year.

Same goes for the taxi driver who, when you arrive at your destination, slowly counts out your change, giving you the note first before fishing about in his canvas bag for the £1.30 change so that you often say, "Don't worry about it mate".

I'll give you another example. You come to buy my car that's up for £5,000 in *Auto Trader*. You visit and I let you have a test drive and look around, and then you decide to try a cheeky offer, "I'll give you £3,000 for it".

If I put my hand out straightaway and shake on it, give you a big smile and say "Deal", how would you feel as you drive home?

What's going through your head?

"Shit, what's wrong with it?"

Or, "I could have gone even cheaper".

When selling, be careful of this. I'm not a negotiator, I'm just not, but I know there are times when sales are sometimes not about price. Instead it's about value and confidence.

Paying the right price gives people confidence.

On Twitter, BUY MY STUFF type tweets are the social media equivalent of mustard gas.

In networking events those people that just drone on and on about how great their product/service is lose everyone's interest.

@PhilTerrett of the appreciation marketing agency, Philosophics, said:

> The three best ways to get business are:
>
> 1 More business from existing customers.
> 2 Recovering past customers.
> 3 Through referrals from people who genuinely know us. So why do we spend so much time chasing people we don't know for new business? The easy answer is that (at least theoretically) it's a numbers game. The more people we meet/email/follow/like, the more people will buy from us, and this should always be a part of any marketing strategy.
>
> However, spare a thought for the people we already know and work with. They have already decided that they like us enough to do business with us – why not give them the encouragement they need to do more with us. Appreciation marketing is about creating the conditions that will enable that to happen, through regular personal contact.

Meet + Like + Know + Trust + Requirement + Price is right = Sale

It's that simple. Selling in a networking environment doesn't work – yet we are all there to sell. But it's counterintuitive.

Stand up and be heard or sit down and be ignored. Both are your choice.

So how do you position things?

I'm afraid you have a 40% chance of failing or you have a 60% chance of success. Basic glass half full stuff. So why not always go with the bigger number?

You know the first time I met my wife in a nightclub, I never said, "Hi, want to come back to my place for sex and in the morning we'll get married and in nine months we'll move in and have a family and in 15 years' time you'll hate me?"

Ridiculous isn't it, although as it happened, it only took about two weeks.

But the point I'm trying to make here is if I had approached Kerry on that basis on that first night, she'd have run a mile, thinking what a complete nutcase I was.

Same goes for sales. I've seen perfectly smart people, with amazing products, totally lose a sale or blow a newly-formed relationship by going in like an enthusiastic teenager.

I'm at a networking meeting, and a guy comes in late huffing and puffing about how the traffic was terrible etc., which would be fine, but then he stands up during the introduction round and says, "My name is Steve and I run a virtual personal assistant company. We do the jobs you hate and make your business and time more efficient".

Erm, really?

You have to be the brand; *you* have to be the business. I'm sure I wasn't the only person from the 20 in the room that didn't miss the irony of the situation.

Or how about the fat hypnotherapist that deals with weight loss.

How does that work?

It doesn't.

If you want to be credible – be the product.

Would either of those examples instil you with confidence?

Of course not.

So if I'm saying never trust a skint telemarketer and that's exactly what you are, then we need to do something about that.

Stop being skint, by selling the thing you claim you are amazing at.

My mate @MarkyMedia got a job shooting and editing a video. The job was billed out at £6,000 film production and editing (one-day shoot) which sounds a bit pricey. But when you find out that it's a two-man team, a drive to Cardiff from Newcastle, a hotel stop, fuel and so on, it is in fact really good value.

And that's what I'm proposing you do. Never put in a quote without flagging up exactly what it's for.

Once you start totting it up and spelling it out for your clients, you get a greater chance of securing a YES:

- Film production and editing (one-day shoot).
- Two-man team.
- £150 fuel.

- £100 hotel.
- Driving time (8 hours).
- £30,000 of equipment.
- 10 years of experience.
- Two days of editing.

In lieu of having a *Star Trek* transporter, getting to destinations to undertake jobs takes time.

All of a sudden what may have seemed a bit expensive now actually sounds pretty reasonable. How you say things makes a massive difference to the outcome.

Get everything in order so that when selling you have supreme confidence in your offering. It's absolutely essential. The person sat opposite you is buying confidence, your confidence that you can do exactly what you say you can.

This is crucial when you are selling.

Start looking at things from your customer's perspective when talking to a potential client. Make sure the words you say are steered towards what they are *hearing*.

4Networking Network Director, Stef Thomas @NoRed-Braces, highlighted this to me in a great way. He took a bottle of water from his bag and said, "See, Evian has got a problem. I realised this when I walked into a Total garage the other day and looked at the cold drinks display in front of me.

There was Evian at £1.19 a bottle alongside other brands like Buxton and Volvic, all of which were cheaper and all of which are basically the same combination of hydrogen and oxygen atoms with some trace minerals." Stef did A Level Chemistry in 1988 and sometimes he likes to show off.

"The problem is that they need us to decide to buy *their* bottle even though it is more expensive. The way they attack this problem really interests me.

They don't have a salesperson standing next to the fridge pointing out the features and benefits of their brand of water nor do they have a brochure for you to read prior to making a decision. They have seconds to make an impact on you before you work out that what is in that bottle is actually more expensive than what you just filled your car up with.

So they go for visual impact and make themselves attractive to you, quite subtly and very cleverly. They tint the bottle blue, because when you see blue water you are unconsciously reminded of cool streams and the sort of clear mountain water you have seen in films.

They put some mountain decals around the top of the bottle, further reinforcing the notion that the water is bottled by shepherds high up on a glacier mountain somewhere. They put a photo of an attractive young person wearing casual and fashionable clothes on the front because, of course, drinking their water will make you healthier and most likely more attractive to the opposite sex. And in a final flourish they make the specially designed 'sports cap' bright red, making certain that that cap and not the other bottles is the very first thing you notice in the fridge."

So how is this relevant to us when we get up in the morning and decide to go out networking?

It's because we have exactly the same problem. And yet we don't have Evian's massive marketing budget.

We have to be noticed for all the right reasons. See, everything we do when we go networking is putting a wrapper around us. Everything we do becomes our Evian bottle, whether we want it to or not.

People notice much more than we think and people DO make snap judgements, as much as we advise them not to in networking circles. Know this and use it to your advantage.

Think about what you want people to think of you and make sure you're that person. If you run a personal assistant business, how do you want to be perceived? Punctual? Organised? Efficient? So make sure that is how you are.

What about a presentation skills coach? You'd better make sure your introduction is the best one in the room.

An expert on sales and marketing? Practice what you preach – you can't be scared to follow up and close.

I've seen the most convincing presentations ruined by people not being the person that they talked about and I've seen people's presentations massively enhanced when they did.

Same goes for *Ground Floor Opportunities!* Every month I am asked to get involved in the next big thing in Multi-Level Marketing (MLM) – with the introducers telling people how much they *will* earn. If you want to be plausible, tell them how much you *are* earning.

I'm really not interested in MLM as I no longer have any inclination to waterski behind a yacht . . .

So if you are that IFA with the dicky service lights and you really can't afford to get them fixed, take the bulbs out.

So what have you learned?

LIFE:

BUSINESS:

IDEAS:

Is your life/business likely to be that little bit easier? Y / N

10

IT'S ONLY AN AMBUSH IF YOU DON'T KNOW IT'S THERE

Great leaders have to make decisions.

Decisions that not everyone will like.

That's great leaders for you.

Everyone has their own ideas, agendas and hidden agendas and as a result we are always in a state of flux.

You would think you could reach a point in your life or business when drama is no more and stability wins through.

It does, but then trouble comes your way again.

The first lesson is that if you want to make progress in your life, not everyone is going to keep up with you.

You are going to lose people along the way.

You are not going to be able to convince those people that don't like you to like you. So don't waste your life.

Equally, when running a business, if you do find yourself trying to get everyone to like you, you'll end up slowing down your progress or even worse anchoring yourself and wrapping yourself up in knots to appease everyone.

Sometimes just through circumstance, stuff happens which turns good friends into good enemies. But then, worse than that, these new enemies can start working on mutual friends to change their opinion of you too. Understand this – you could be Mahatma Gandhi and someone would still want to put a bullet in your head for your views on world peace.

Regardless of who you are, you are going to have seven knobheads who try to negatively muscle their way into your life. OK, some may not like those words, but it's undoubtedly the most succinct way to sum up what I'm talking about.

Those *competitors* that rubbish *every* positive thing you do, those that go out of their way to work against you. Remember the seminal Hanna Barbera cartoon hit *Wacky Races*, the kind of people who would turn a FINISH LINE *This Way* arrow the opposite way whilst twisting their baddie's moustache.

You are going to have seven. Count 'em.

They'll whisper your successes, yet shout all your failures.

These people come in many forms, but the really dangerous ones will appear to be well-meaning and act like they are trying to help you.

It's only an ambush if you don't know it's there.

I was on the same bill as an author and speaker called @MikeSouthon, who did a corking presentation all about Richard Branson. Mike had interviewed him live on stage at various events.

Throughout his presentation, he ran a few montage videos of Branson in action, including the Virgin Group Showreel as well as material on Virgin Galactic, his space adventure and Virgin Unite, his not-for-profit venture.

After Mike played the footage, he said, "What do you think?", as he suggested the video would have reaffirmed whatever view people had of Branson.

This was his point, that everyone has strong views on Branson, some (like me and Mike) feel he is a charismatic visionary, who's had many successes and is an all-round good egg.

While other people have a different view – they see him as a ruthless, oafish, egotistical idiot.

Mike explained that whichever side of the fence you sit, your view would be reaffirmed, not changed, by watching the promo video.

The same goes for me – OK, I'm not Branson for a start off and I certainly don't have the hair, but my attention-grabbing approach is similar.

Often when we look at people, it's our pre-existing view of them that clouds our judgement and nothing can change that.

You are never going to be able to appease everyone, so stop trying, know that what you are doing is for the right reasons. Your reasons. It's like reading a magazine – sensible people just turn over the pages on articles they have no interest in, whereas knobheads will waste their time drafting ANGRY "DEAR SIR" LETTERS to the editor, or the modern version which involves:

TYPING CAPITAL LETTERS FURIOUSLY WITH TWO FINGERS ON LINKED IN BLOGS.

Please note: this kind of activity does not pay your mortgage.

Stop wasting your valuable life trying to convince people that you are a good person. Successful people do not use time, energy or resource on things they cannot control.

Talkers. Doers. Whingers.

Which are you?

The only person that really matters in all of this is you. If you can look at yourself in the mirror each day, sleep easy each night you place your head on your pillow, knowing that you are doing the right thing, that's what matters.

You can get blown about by this stuff or choose to concentrate on the good fight.

There are the kind of people who get offended by a swearword on my Twitter timeline – I call them the "Victorian Wife brigade" – fainting then needing smelling salts to come back around. Stay away from those who are outraged at nothings, those who try to undermine your ambitions. Be the one that supports someone else's ambitions. Knobheads that work to undermine a particular leader seem surprised when their opinion is then dismissed as irrelevant by that same leader. A networking bugbear of mine is when people *cufflink*, talking bullshit for the sake of sounding *professional*. In my profession I encounter people all the time like this. A classic you'll hear in networking circles is, "I need bigger businesses".

Promise me reader, the minute someone says that to you, please fire out this question – "Are you a bigger business?"

No.

"Well piss off, *as I need bigger businesses.*"

Everyone has value, not just the person you are talking to, but all the people they know, never forget that.

A sales trainer told me he was not interested in working with smaller companies. Ironically I heard he was then badmouthing a competitor who had 15 small companies paying £99 a piece, which is actually £500 more than the £1000 he would get from his target big company.

Don't torpedo opportunity by being *that* person.

Making genuine friends in business generally means making genuine money in business. But if the purpose of making friends is to make money, it somehow doesn't quite work. These people can fill you with fear, stress, self-doubt.

If you listen to them. Once you boil it down, what is the risk? Death? Nope. Starvation? Nope. Losing your house? A long way to go from the minute a snotty letter lands.

There are few situations in life or business that are insurmountable.

You make the decisions for your life, so don't let others place a set of negative values on you. Stop listening to them, remove these people from your life, don't waste time attempting to convince people who don't like you of your benign intent, you can't win that one.

Keep your head, keep your focus and trust, that what you are doing is part of your mission, to make a positive difference to your life and those that matter.

I had a really informed conversation with a top business psychologist/NLP expert in his field. He told me the reason why successful people get haters, critics and blamers who take great pleasure cultivating drama, well beyond what would be considered rational behaviour.

A great example of this is those internet trolls who TYPE FURIOUSLY.

He suggested I do some research on the "Drama Triangle", which I did. It makes for some serious reading and meant that for the first time ever, I now have an insight into why peeps spew out disproportionate venom and poison.

The model posits three habitual psychological roles (or role-plays) which people often take in a situation:

1 The person who plays the role of a Victim.
2 The person who pressures, coerces or Persecutes the victim.
3 The Rescuer, who intervenes, seemingly out of a desire to help the situation or the underdog.

The Victim is not really as helpless as he feels, the Rescuer is not really helping, and the Persecutor does not really have a valid complaint.

SOURCE: Wikipedia

Google "Drama Triangle" to help stop yourself from getting roped in.

Leave the bad behaviour to the other side.

You may have people like that in your life. You may have to cut these people off or at the very least be more aware of your exposure to them on your way to an easier life and business.

Have a think about those around you (sometimes it's even your own family) who you just have to create enough distance between that it doesn't create problems.

My entire social circle has changed massively and even before I discovered the Drama Triangle, I recognised that there are people who no longer factor in my plans for breaking through.

It doesn't mean you don't love, like or care for these people. It just means that you can't save everyone. But you can save yourself from a world of drama and negativity by moving away from it.

I shared war stories with Mike after the event and he told me a story about when he spoke at a conference for IFAs, with over 1,500 people in the room. The response from the audience was a positive one, with 100+ positive feedback forms completed, with just one that stood out.

The form had "POOR" circled.

As a perfectionist, Mike was wounded by this and spent time trying to work out what he could have done to have made the delegate circle EXCELLENT instead of POOR.

The answer is, nothing.

Some people are never happier than when they've just missed the bus.

People *will* criticise your work. You are never going to be able to make everyone happy or agree with all your decisions.

The trick is not to let one negative comment wipe out all the good you achieve each and every day.

@debbiehuxton said she was concerned about some of the things being said online about me in one teeny corner of the internet – seven knobheads. Turns out, it was a forum with seven people in an echo chamber, all endlessly agreeing with each other that everything I did was terrible.

I said, "Debbie, do you remember a time when you worked in A&E ward as a green, student nurse, when your first emergency came through, at times going literally green with the things you were dealing with? It's overwhelming, creating confusion and panic. But then as time went on, dealing with that sort of stuff became second nature".

This is going to be crucial in your journey – working through those down days when things don't go your way, when you feel absolutely shitty and then to top it off you get some unnecessary, uninvited, uncalled for salvos of ill feelings, sent express delivery.

You won't appreciate them at first, nothing could be worse at that moment, but in time it'll all make complete sense.

Those that matter, matter. Those that don't, don't.

It's like conditioning your resolve.

@AceOfWaste, "It's the universe's way of finding out if you believe in your vision".

There's a long way to go from the minute bullets of negativity start whizzing overhead, so don't waste your time looking for the white flag.

When someone has done their worst and that's not taken you out, everything that follows is just gonna bounce off you.

No matter how great you are, no matter how noble your deeds, not everyone is going to like you. That's life.

Think about it logically . . . It's because you are winning.

And the seven want you to lose.

Keep on winning.

Roy Hurley (www.heldereng.com) is bang on:

Why people are so different is that we all carry our own model of the universe around in our head. How to walk, talk, the ability to predict danger, how things work and why things work are all simulated in our brains. This helps us to predict and function in a complicated world, everything from gravity to relationships are all reproduced in a working model in the brain.

Now there is only one universe and one set of rules.

But everyone's model is very, very different. Everyone's model is broken, missing rules and just plain wrong in areas. That's because people can only build it on their own life experience and so it's shaped by how they understand and process that experience. So, we are really all living in different realities. It's more of a miracle that we can agree on anything rather than be exasperated at our profound differences.

Turn down the volume on negative influences in your life and replace them with positive ones. People will make rules for others and exceptions for themselves. I see opportunities frittered away because someone chose to listen to someone who had their agenda at the forefront.

Make your own mind up about people and don't listen to negative stories about others.

Those feeding you stories put their own agenda first, not yours. People are entitled to not like you, your business or what you stand for. That's life. No matter how serious you believe a drama is, at some point, it will be tomorrow's chip paper. So step away from the Drama Triangle and no longer seek out or hear those negative voices. People loaded with malice or hidden agendas don't deserve to have time spent listening to them.

Use your time to keep ploughing and moving towards your goals.

Beat them, by being better. Silence them by not quitting.

People under immense pressure or stress will look everywhere else for the source of their problems.

Tip: look first at yourself.

So what have you learned?

LIFE:

BUSINESS:

IDEAS:

Is your life/business likely to be that little bit easier? Y / N

11
WE LOSE SO MANY TODAYS WORRYING ABOUT TOMORROW

If you didn't earn another penny from this moment on, how long would it be before you were in big trouble?

How much do you need to earn to live on Tesco's *Value* beans and waffles?

These are the opening questions that I ask business owners whom I mentor.

I get a fast feel as to where they are financially right now.

Generally when we transition from a regular corporate wage to self-employment, the long weekend breaks of walking around the olive groves of Valencia are over, as is Tarquin's private education.

That's gone, unless you've got savings – but they can dissipate at the same rate as your self-belief.

Well it should be gone. But sometimes we continue to live in the same mindset and financial spend as when we were employed. Mistake.

Instead of full concentration on the business, people focus on maintaining appearances and lifestyle. Some will fast track themselves into an early grave through the self-induced stress caused by trying to keep up with the neighbour's *new plate* car and garden water feature.

Live within your means. Be content with what you have right now, today.

Downsizing your life is crucial when getting your business underway as it helps remove added pressure. You need that all-important mental bandwidth available.

When things start going your way, then get the stuff you want.

Can't be arsed working today and want to have a day off? Do it. You don't even have a boss to ring to pretend to be sick. Equally, want to work at 11pm in the evening, sure, do it.

Don't let others' template of what is appropriate blow you about.

As I mention in Chapter 4, we've been programmed to be mentally chained to a desk between 9 and 5 pressing f5 (send/receive) waiting for emails, based on our corporate conditioning.

Don't be constrained by this idea of conventional work patterns – work 100% when you feel 100% in work mode and if you can't be arsed, go relax or do something else.

It's not the hours that you work, it's your output. That's true work/life balance for you.

Back with our friend @debbiehuxton

This particular shift a patient was brought in by ambulance. I recognised him immediately as he had been in the department several times over the previous few months. He was terminally ill and suffering from cancer. Often with terminally ill patients their immune system has been weakened due to the nature of their treatment and they become susceptible to infection and this was true in this patient's case.

This admission was different though, as he was now at the end stage of his illness and his death was imminent. He had refused to go into a hospice and had no family to support him. He had lost them through his years of alcoholism, twinned with a refusal to accept he was an alcoholic and do anything about this mind and body-rotting illness.

When he finally did make the decision to give up the booze and make some changes in his life, his support system, his nearest and dearest family and friends, was now the sum total of zero – they all had made the decision to leave and his relationships had become toxic due to his out-of-control behaviour and lack of accountability for his own life.

I had grown fond of this patient as I had nursed him many times as his immune system became weaker and weaker and he attended A&E more frequently. This time would be the last time I would nurse him. His body was worn out, he had no more fight left in him, he had accepted defeat. He was a personable guy and we had shared many long conversations about the meaning of life and how he had come to be alone.

(Continued)

He accepted things may have been different if he had made choices to take accountability sooner. Once he had made the decision to move to a life of sobriety, three months later he was diagnosed with pancreatic cancer. He had faced the biggest battle of his life with dignity and much soul searching. As I looked after him on this final shift he was in and out of consciousness, his breathing shallow.

I made him as comfortable as possible and ensured he was pain free. As I moved his head on the pillow, his eyes opened and he smiled weakly at me. He placed his hand on my wrist and said, "Give me your hand". As we held hands he said, "Thank you, Debbie. Thank you for never judging me and for making me feel whole again". I replied, "Thank you for being an amazing patient". His response was to blow my mind.

"Debs, this is it for you and I right now, so will you make me a promise?" I agreed.

"When I die you will be there, and when you leave this shift, please make it the one you make the decision to leave and go run that business you always talked to me about. Go and put you and your wonderful family first!"

Tingles ran all over my body and a deep resolution reared up with the most ferocious courage inside me. Tears stung my cheeks as I nodded silently, unable to speak. He continued:

"As the sun rises tomorrow morning Debs, think of me. With every blade of grass you see, every bird you hear sing, your children's laughter, every time your husband says that he loves you, think of me. Keep my spirit alive and don't let my life have been in vain".

The compassion that coursed through every fibre of my body at that moment was a feeling that has never left me. In that moment something changed inside me.

A doorway opened to a new world.

A few hours later, Dave – he deserves to have his name mentioned at this point – slipped away peacefully at just 40 years old, with me at his side as he took his last breath and the monitors slowed showing the life ebbing from his body. As the monitor showed a flat line I held him in my arms and, professionally or not, I kissed him on his forehead and said the words "I love you" softly in his ear.

Everyone deserves to feel loved and at the end of his short life (he was only my age), he could leave this earth feeling compassion and hearing those words for the last time. When I recount that story now, I feel as passionate now as I did that day in making the decision to leave my job.

Something you should know about Dave's earlier life – he was a barrister, a successful one, earning £150,000+ a year. Working so hard, he ended up drinking, masking the problems of his life. He slid towards becoming an alcoholic who, when drunk, would get aggressive, angry and lash out. It was this which ultimately ended up losing his marriage, family, home, job and finally his life.

Think about that, you don't become a barrister without many years of study – this was someone who had both intelligence and opportunity.

He swapped one bar for another. He didn't just wake up one day to find he had lost it all – you don't just become an alcoholic with seven days of drinking. This happened over time, it just sneaked up on him . . . slowly.

40" waist trousers don't just grow to 42" overnight.

Jay (from Rado watch fame) runs an international video games company. He said, "Some people will get that 'Eureka' moment, that lightbulb on their head that tells them categorically that they have to make a change." For others it's more subtle. Don't ever forget the strength of belief and let it make you part of its plan. Become a "yes" person. Agree to things and see where they take you. Think about how previous "yes's" have changed people's lives and yet they're still gun-shy to say "yes" again.

Ask yourself right now, what decisions are you putting off making?

We have all started down a path, maybe drinking a little too much, smoking, taking drugs or overeating to mask the problems in our life, and before we know it, the masking is now creating more problems than it once blotted out.

What changes are you resisting?

Before you judge a person, remember everyone has a story. Everyone has gone through something that has changed them or their direction.

Sometimes negatively, sometimes positively.

I'm at a trade show in Liverpool and these two guys are talking to the team on our stand. Five minutes in, one of our team introduces them to me, as they were struggling.

"So tell me about this network," they say, when I know they've already been told everything about the network. I ask, "What's the real question?"

"How could we sell to all your members?" I said, "What's the product?" "Well, we don't want to tell you that. In all fairness, we've just met you and you could copy it and go to market with it."

There then follows literally 10 minutes of this back and forth. It was like a *Monty Python* sketch, except this wasn't supposed to be comedy. It was a business approach, a really bad one.

I handed them one of my 4Networking brochures. I said, "There you go, you've now got everything you need to go make a multi-million pound international business."

Just call it 5Networking to avoid any confusion.

If you are so scared of someone running off with your idea tomorrow that you don't do it today what's the point?

You'll always make progress if you're putting one foot in front of the other. But if you are scared of doing that, then the biggest mistake you'll make is continually fearing you're going to make one. The only thing to stop you is you!

Successful people don't waste time on things they have no control over.

The lesson?

That you are never going to make any progress if all you are doing each day is looking for the holes in every bucket of opportunity you come across.

The faux anticipation is worse than the reality. I've been to meetings where people insist on spending money on Non-Disclosure Agreements (NDAs).

Not once have I signed a single one placed in front of me. Honestly, my life and business is OK without having to hear your amazing idea. Thanks.

Each time I have refused to sign.

And each of those five times, the person opposite me has reluctantly accepted and then told me what the master plan is, without me signing an NDA.

I am not prepared to sign something to have a meeting.

The truth is that not one of the ideas that was pitched by the person sat in front of me clutching their unsigned NDA was so groundbreaking that in my opinion was worth spending the £500 on the legals.

This isn't Silicon Valley, you are not Apple. An idea is 1%. The doing it is the 99%. Lots of people want to dick about and re-dick about on the 1%.

Have a think about some of your old, learnt behaviour and business teachings that you are carrying. In today's hyper-lean, super manoeuverable world they may no longer be fit for purpose.

My life changed when I stopped smoking weed, just as I started 4Networking in 2006. I took the hazy pot filter off my life, stopped using it to mask the problems in my life. They were still there, but the difference was I was in a much stronger position to deal with them.

Faith and fear never go in the same direction. Make up your mind which way you want to go. Don't over-think a situation. This is what clogs up your mental bandwidth, slows you down and makes you over-compensate, seeing shadows that actually may not exist. Are those granite kitchen work surfaces you want really worth a heart attack?

Things that seem like a good idea today can cause us a whole lot more problems tomorrow.

So what have you learned?

LIFE:

BUSINESS:

IDEAS:

Is your life/business likely to be that little bit easier? Y / N

12

BUILD IT AND THEY WILL COME. SOMETIMES.

This only works if what you build is something people can't get a better version of elsewhere . . . or in today's world on eBay or Amazon.

People will pay for quality. Gaucho, Disney, Apple, Virgin Active, 4Networking . . .

As a business, do you know what you are? Do you know the position you hold in your field?

My job involves me driving all over the UK, spending numerous nights away. I'm always looking for examples of great and terrible customer service.

95% of the time I stay in budget hotels.

Back in the bad old days of employment, when someone else was picking up the tab, I, as an *executive*, would be OUTRAGED if my overnight accommodation was anything less than 4 star.

Now, when I actually pay for my own hotels, it's £39 Travelodges. *Lovely*.

It's true, I actually do love them. There's something basic yet clean and Zen-like about them. The idea of taking the wife away for a romantic weekend break to one probably wouldn't work, but arriving at 11.30pm and then out the door at 7am, it's a bed, it's all you need.

There is a time and a place for everything.

On the night before I was due to deliver a keynote speech at the Business North West Show at the Manchester Central Exhibition Centre, as is customary, I went out for eats with the then MD of the show's organising company @ScottHider. It was my shout, and he suggested we could get a nice steak @gauchogroup. Table booked, we arrived to be shown to our table.

I remember looking at the funky cowhide chairs. Everything, including the menu, exuded quality. That was before I opened the menu, which when I did nearly caused me to spit out my mineral water.

It was around £25 for a steak, which I chose from the waitress when she brought to the table a big thick and no doubt expensive wooden chopping board where she described each of the cuts, and sold in how beautifully each piece of meat was aged for 28 days. If you've never been, probably the best way to describe it is it's like a lap-dancing club for steak. Oh, you've never been to a lap-dancing club . . . me neither.

*Ahem, back to Gaucho. After you've chosen your meat, you then get the added bonus of being in for £5 for a dainty "bucket" of chips!

Customers will pay for *razzle dazzle*. The show.

Scott said, "Trust me". My whining went on until the smiley waitress returned with my just-how-I-like-it steak, well done . . . I took my first mouthful and tasted it.

Scott was 100% right. The reason the young waitress could tell me about each cut of meat wasn't because she had an interest in them, but that she had been trained to *look* like she had an interest in them. She was knowledgeable enough to be able to answer all the likely questions she'd be asked.

Since then I've never looked back and whenever I have a reason to celebrate a big business success, Gaucho it is.

Want to impress a new client. Gaucho.

Celebrating being signed to Wiley for this book. Gaucho.

The last time I took a friend to Gaucho on my suggestion was a Monday evening in Leeds. She also went through the same *mumble mumble* nonsense, as I did whilst looking through the menu, until she tasted the steak.

After we finished the meal, I made my way back to where my car was parked, walking past another national steak house restaurant. There was not one single customer sat down.

Not one.

Remember, I'd just left an *expensive* steak restaurant where we had to wait 20 minutes before getting a table.

We can convince ourselves there's a recession on and that cheaper is better and exactly what the client wants. In some capacity it is, price is always going to be the key factor, unless the customer wants quality.

You can turn the staunchest of unbelievers into fans, if you can get them to taste the steak.

That's not a euphemism.

There is a market for cheap. There is also a market for the quality your business offers. But during those periods when our belief is eroded, we convince ourselves that times are hard and there's an economic downturn etc. etc., so we talk ourselves out of things and in turn we create the reality and the problem we are trying to avoid.

As part of my research of this book, I spent a week in California. It's a tough job I know, but three of those days were training at the Disney Institute, their corporate training arm. It was important to get an insight into how such a world-class organisation operates, how it develops its best practice and what lessons I could take away for my own business. Guess what, it wasn't cheap.

Did you know, at all Disney parks, every flower is replaced each month – that is why they always look just perfect.

Every lightbulb is replaced at 60% of its manufacturer's suggested lifetime.

Why? Because a blown lightbulb sends the wrong message. That lack of attention to detail could spoil the dream of a perfect day and that would have Walt spinning in his cryogenically frozen sarcophagus.

Ignoring the small details of your business can send BIG messages.

Disney started with a mouse. As an idea, vision and belief.

Imagine if Uncle Walt had told people his organisation would one day achieve even 1/1000th of its current success. He would have been locked away in a loony bin.

It helps, if like me, you are half-mental enough to have such an outrageous goal the likes of which others laugh at you.

Now Disney employs hundreds of thousands of people all over the world in their TV channels, theme parks, merchandising, music, films, property, cruises, training arm, Disney Institute. The list goes on and on . . .

Annual profits in the billions. BILLIONS.

Disney make no excuses, their product IS expensive. It's supposed to be.

It's also the best in its field.

Top-class businesses place you right in the middle of the experience, and like Walt Disney started with a mouse, your business should also start with something simple . . .

The customer.

Same goes for Apple products, of which I'm a massive fan. Hey, maybe your Android is a better platform, it's a subjective matter. But what I can say, with complete certainty, is when I bought my iPad at the Apple store in Bristol, I had had 362 trouble-free days of ownership before dropping it and breaking the screen when I was in the US.

I arranged an appointment at a local Apple store to see how much it would cost to get it fixed.

Within three minutes of being at the store, the assistant tapped in my iPad's serial code and said, "Hey no problem sir, accidents happen, I'll get you a replacement", followed by a lovely Florida "You're welcome". Ten minutes later I was back in my car.

My fault, yet they fixed my problem at their cost.

Try doing that with your Android thingamabob.

I got a wireless printer for my primary home PC, and after spending over an hour downloading and installing the drivers to set it up, I failed to get it working. Once the frustration really kicked in, I thought I'd give it one last try. Still nothing.

Then I remembered the brand new iMac in the other room, although to be honest I'd not really got my head around transitioning from Windows to Mac just yet.

I thought I'd give it a whirl.

Two minutes later, it's online and printing.

There's a great business lesson here, that heritage, brand loyalty and goodwill can only carry you so far before an easier alternative is looked for.

I don't know how much research and development spend is needed to make this wireless printer magic happen, but someone, somewhere within the Apple organisation authorised and signed a cheque in the department of *Make Brad's Printer Work Wireless Instantly*, so that he will be blown away.

Of course that's not what happened, but that's how I felt.

Onto my gym now, Virgin Active. I know very little about the management, but Branson has put his name to it, so that's a good start. But what I do know is that they do everything right – well OK, they *try* to do everything right.

After a gym session, I was between meetings and sat in their lobby, listening to their membership sales team doing their thing and I was totally blown away, just absolutely ooh la la. Laughing at the punters' jokes, the laughs sounded and *almost* looked real.

In the hour or so I sat there, they conducted five walk-arounds and signed three new members. That's special.

Life. Business. Just got easier.

There is just something unique about an organisation which primarily has young staff permeating fun and yet which never loses sight of the serious commercial element.

Looking at every detail, from the facilities and cheerful staff, to the funky red-branded designer gymwear uniform, they don't appear to cut corners. As a punter that's encouraging.

But it's more than that – they have created a culture where everyone can feel welcome. There are no meatheads staring daggers, the ethos doesn't allow it. I'm sure the staff are trained to deter that kind of behaviour by using those big cheery smiles and talking nothings to defuse anyone walking in with an attitude.

It's a joy to see. That's why they can charge me £65 a month compared to the £30 at my local spit and sawdust independent gym.

Oh, and also, the membership allows me full access to all 120 Virgin Active clubs across the UK, perfect for me as I travel around the country. So it's not just one thing, it's how it all comes together, how each cog within the team plays its part so it all just works.

OK, I'm now being a bit cheeky putting my own business 4Networking alongside these great examples, but it's my aspiration to make my organisation as great at the companies I've just written about.

In a field of many others in your sector, how do you stand out? You have to be different – different works. In my business we've chosen to offer a "4Networking Passport" which allows our members to attend any of the 5,000+ networking meetings we run each year across the UK. That's totally unique. Yet it now seems such an obvious benefit to offer.

An organisation's culture has to start somewhere, and it should begin with the leader sharing his or her vision about what is right for their business's target market. How different would my company be if I was a pinstripe suit-wearing former banker with a much more conventional and reserved approach.

The whole look, feel and vibe throughout would be unrecognisable.

Would you even be reading *this* book?

You have to start somewhere. Your culture is defined by you, its leader. Be the best you can be.

As it all starts with you.

A membership org without memberships means you've got no org. A company without customers won't be a company for very long.

People join 4Networking. People leave 4Networking.

Same goes for you and your business. You are going to lose clients, but don't beat yourself up over it. As long as you gain more than you lose that's OK, that's business. You can't keep everyone.

You can be the architect of your own business, but there are times when you should be prepared to also be the builder, delivery driver and plumber.

We are seeing the death of complex business models. Simplicity is the key. Make it easy for people to say "Yes". Remove the hurdles.

Remember the darts club of old – fat blokes smoking and drinking in front of a small crowd. Then someone along the way said, "Hey, let's make darts sexy".

Another candidate for the loony bin until you see that the arenas are now packed out. It's more like a gladiatorial boxing match. They've somehow made an old fat blokes' sport look cool and, escorted by two cheerleaders, look sexy.

Someone made that decision, that call to go against everything that had gone before and they pulled it off. I think maybe I'll get some dry ice and get a couple of Spearmint Rhino cheerleaders walking me into my speaking gigs.

Why not? Because I'm not 50, fat and a darts player. Yet.

Mediocrity in life, in business. Do you really want that? I certainly don't. You don't want mediocre service, TV, relationships, health. So don't expect others to forgo the same checks that you are doing.

Ask yourself this – if you were your customer, would your approach work and appeal to you?

If not, then you should change it to something that would.

Why do so many companies make life so difficult for themselves and, worse than that, for their potential customers?

I see it all the time in business.

The other day I visited a hotel that proudly displayed a sign saying "FREE WIFI".

"Brill," I thought. "I'll have a bit of that."

I had to ask at reception for the key needed in order to access the FREE WIFI. They give me a printed piece of paper containing the "simple" key code I had to enter. This is it (and I quote):

```
451F20A406FAD8fF5C34EDa4441BEE855DF691C
9809633d1414
```

And when I say "enter", I mean I had to put it in twice. That's right, boys and girls. No cutting and pasting of WEP keys. Twice.

Note that this particular key is also laced with lowercasers for that added IT comedic effect.

Here it is again:

```
451F20A406FAD8fF5C34EDa4441BEE855DF691C
9809633d1414
```

Several failed tries later I reached for my MiFi dongle and got online that way.

I'm no technical geek but surely to God it's possible to have a sensible password like "Lobby1" or something a bit quirky like "woohoo"? What a customer service gaffe.

You promise free WiFi, but are so scared to death that someone who is not buying coffee and having a bite to eat in your lounge may be sat in a car outside your hotel downloading porn on your FREE bandwidth.

As a result you turn a relative non issue into one that now has paranoid-induced military-grade encryption security, the likes of which would normally be found in a CIA *Special Projects* mainframe.

What has happened to good old customer service?

I went to a well-known American diner in the Midlands the other day, you'll know it. Back in the early 90s, this brand was more than just food. It was an "experience", something to talk about to others.

Now though, the food for what it is, is overpriced and that once authentic American Diner Experience was nowhere to be found.

It kind of looked the same but there was no effort to make the food appetizing – the pictures on the menu looked much better than it tasted. Back in the day, they tasted just like they looked.

Or maybe they never did, maybe it's because I've grown up now.

Ordering some cocktails, they were served in BIG thick-rimmed glasses with enough ice to sink the *Titanic*. "Cocktail cost-saving No 101: quick, let's jip the paying customer."

It just wasn't even done cleverly. It's only magic if you don't see how it's done.

The shareholders may well be pleased this year when the dividends are issued, but that's me done. You have lost a former fan and advocate.

As I said earlier, their model maybe allows for it – there'll always be a new customer who will not know any better. Perhaps I'm seeing things through blinkered eyes, but where's the "experience" gone? Or maybe my best chili beef nachos days are behind me, and as a 40 year old it's now all about a £30 steak, £5 chips and a £3 peppercorn sauce.

It's only too expensive if you want it but can't afford it.

Going back to mentals – when I got my business moving in those early days with little resource, I did the things that most normal people wouldn't. Like talking to myself!

Talking to myself on our online forums when they launched, I'd set up alternative accounts and be switching between them. Think of it like going on a pub crawl – you walk into an empty pub, turn around and go onto the next one which is busy.

You have to be busy, to be busy.

A business leader needs to transition and adapt and grow with the business, in the same way a fish will only grow as big as its tank allows. If you are going to have a top-class business you need to be able to grow on every front: thinking, vision and belief.

I met with the director of a sheet fabrication company, which had been sat at £250,000 turnover for the last 10 years. The management had no ideas, no vision, no belief.

It's not like he chose to keep the business at this level and was off playing golf and enjoying life each day. No, he was now a 60 year old, lugging metal about and barely keeping his company and six staff afloat. The risk-averse nature of the leadership meant they had made no progress, simply pegging the business where it was. Staying right smack bang in the middle of that continued stress zone.

It was no surprise when he told me, "The climate is tough". There's a reason it's been tough for the entire life span of his business.

Occasionally decisions you make for your business will see a revolt from your customers as some may not like it. Yet if you are gaining more than you are losing, then as a leader that's the right decision to make.

In the past we've made changes to our website and these are invariably followed by four days of rants such as, "I'M LEAVING!" Then a week later those same people wake up and "quite like it now".

Some will blame your business for things that are not your fault, like "it's too expensive". It's not – it's just that they can't afford it.

With each of the great businesses I mentioned, what makes them leaders in their fields?

I believe it's the leadership's ability to make decisions that go in their favour and continue to go in their favour. Flipping a coin and getting it right, time after time.

Each of these brands has carved out a niche in a congested, often much cheaper, marketplace by using every trick in the book to elbow themselves into a space that normal thinkers would have called impossible.

It's that attention to detail, getting the smallest of things right and then to keep doing it all the way through, even at times losing money to maintain the image of your brand. Focus on investing in the kinds of things which customers more often than not don't see, but they might.

Then you have big dollops of ethos and training and a culture of informed and considered risk taking.

Quality means if you get it wrong, you do what it takes to get it right.

Leaders who refused to lose, even when they were losing. That's what makes great brands great.

A bit of a left-field one, if you were to align your business in terms of a food outlet, where would you position it? Local kebab shop, McDonald's, local bistro, Indian, Gaucho?

If you were to ask that the same question to your customers, what would they say?

Because if you say Gaucho, yet you are charging local bistro money, something is out of alignment.

Regardless of the size of your current business, by keeping your eyes and ears open on your travels, you are using your time twice. And the lessons you learn each day from observing the way quality companies operate will help you to steer your business into a similar direction.

I am always capturing the things I see on my travels on my iPhone notes app. Rely solely on your memory and you'll forget some real gems. Then once a week, review them, looking for the ways you can apply them to your business and your marketplace.

You can't fully systematise a business that relies on people, but you can show them what the start, the middle and the end should look like.

By now, you should have a better idea of what your business stands for and what sort of leader you are.

Should you come across a lightbulb out within your business, change it as soon as you see it until you have the budgets of the big boys. Probably the same way they had to before they had the success they currently enjoy.

So what have you learned?

LIFE:

BUSINESS:

IDEAS:

Is your life/business likely to be that little bit easier? Y / N

13
EXPERIENCE IS WHAT YOU WIN, WHEN YOU LOSE

Each decision we each make is the correct one, based on our knowledge. Based on our experience.

The greatest activity any business can undertake is one that is low investment, high impact. These are just beautiful. It's like winning on a fruit machine and then getting the opportunity to hold the winning reels and spin again. As your business grows, these present themselves more and more.

In those formative years you are more inclined to do things that make you feel like you are busy, but deep down you know you are dicking about.

HIGH investment, LOW impact tasks. You can always find these things to do.

An example you may recognise is preparing for a presentation. I've yet to see a PowerPoint presentation that actually needed a PowerPoint presentation.

The reason I know this is because I was one of those who would spend days on them, instead of dealing with the thing I should have – my nerves or actually practising.

As the days counted down until my moment of truth/ terror presentation, I'd hide behind my computer screen, manipulate the shapes and transitions of each slide, when the truth was, this activity was a shield for my nerves. Quite rightly nervous, because you don't just gain the ability to speak in front of an audience overnight.

But the more you do of anything, the better you become. I now have a professional speaking career, not as a result of using PowerPoint to create slides, but through the experience gained by speaking over 500 times during the 15-minute 4Sight (insight, not sales pitch) section of my 4Networking meetings. I've taught myself to speak in public, by pushing through the nerves each and every time.

I've not used a PowerPoint presentation in seven years and I do alright.

With anything in your life, as long as you are making progress, even if the only real gain is with learning, then it's good. The danger is when you are perpetually dicking about, and not even gaining confidence.

Roy Hurley (www.heldereng.com) said,

People jump through hoops to avoid discomfort.

They don't want to be too hot, too cold, work too hard, sweat, carry heavy things or confront painful truths. The problem is when you go through life avoiding discomfort, your threshold to tolerate pain and discomfort narrows, creating a constant feedback loop of avoiding and feeling discomfort.

"Grasp the nettle" – embrace pain, discomfort and hard work. It makes you harder, makes comfortable times more pleasurable and gives you back the energy you would have spent dodging discomfort at all costs to do more noble things.

Otherwise known as "take a spoonful of cement and harden up, princess" in my native tongue.

What I didn't mention before, Roy's an Aussie. People who hit their sales targets by the middle of the month, but keep on going like it's the start of the month, have that winning ingredient needed to get momentum.

If I gave you £5,000 to invest in your business, on the understanding that you made £5,001 back, what would you spend it on and how would it help you?

Marketing is the thing you do to make it easier to sell. But I can't think of one sensible marketing initiative where you spend £5,000 and get £5,001 + collateral awareness back.

Not one. I'm not investing anything. I'm making the point that in business spending money is easy, but making money back is much, much harder. This morning, I received an approach by a company offering me a golden ticket to a MEET THE BUYER event. It's tempting to think that all I need to do is get the £5k needed and the contracts and riches will be mine.

The only reason the buyers attend these events is because they are on an all-expenses paid jolly to sit around in a hotel all day, and get shit-faced at the free bar in the evening. These events have been contributed to by the companies daft enough to have paid the £5k to be wheeled in front of each of the buyers, for 20 minutes and laugh at their jokes.

How do I know this? Because many years ago I was one of those buyers.

It's like being a really shitty Father Christmas for the day.

Meeting companies who somehow felt that by just signing a cheque it bought them a jump to the front of some mythical business success queue.

This is not how business is done.

You can read all the books like this in the world, have the best mentors, but ultimately you are going to need the scars that only getting it wrong and experience can give you.

Some people along your journey may act like they are trying to help you.

Offering you a fast track pathway to success. Sometimes it doesn't work out, sometimes it does.

@debbiehuxton found herself faced with an opportunity to gain some big momentum.

In those first few months of running her own business she landed on her feet, with a chance introduction to a business guru. He saw everything that she could be, and told her that with her skills, she could make a whole heap of money. This person would leverage everything that had gone before. Her nursing profession was actually the perfect base for her to start her own business and, for the first time, here was someone who could see all of her potential. All she needed to do in order to fully unlock her greatness, was find the key.

In this case the key was to buy a coaching licence for £7,500.

That's a lot of money – even more so when you don't have it.

Well, it's not really if you earn £100k in the first year as she was assured by this individual she would.

On that basis, it's an absolute bargain!

When it came to decisions, her husband Simon was the sensible one, ruled by the head not the heart, and during the nice meals out with the guru and his family he was constantly evaluating the situation and in turn the guru.

Each time the guru picked them up in his high spec Range Rover, he allowed them a peek through a window to what their future could hold. The glint of his gold Rolex was never lost, and purposely was catching Simon's eye each time the guru turned the steering wheel.

No business like show business.

Whichever way Simon and Debbie look, success was painted. Neither of them considered the licence a risk but instead a shrewd investment.

This was their moment, their once-in-a-lifetime opportunity to break into the big world of business consulting. The big time.

Then came the point when the agreement was signed and the funds were bank transferred, and her saviour was no longer responding to emails. No longer taking her calls. It was clear that her money had gone, along with her dream of being an overnight business success.

The whole thing was a Hollywood film set. A balsa wood reality.

This turned out to be worse than swapping the family cow for three magic beans, as Debbie had remortgaged her house to buy the "licence" which she had been urged to get to unlock the success she deserved for her family.

We can be so blinded because of our hunger for something that it blurs our thinking on how these people operate. They make us talk *ourselves* into believing that somehow the gods have shined on us by granting us the winning hand we now hold.

By all means bet your house on yourself, but betting your house based on what someone you barely know tells you perhaps isn't the wisest of moves.

Regardless of how sweet the Merlot at those initial meetings tastes.

Before you get your chequebook out and embark on a path with your favourite business guru, type their name into Google followed by the word "scam".

If Debbie had done that, she would have saved the £20,000 she ultimately invested in a business that was never likely to have worked from the outset. I can tell you now, in my experience, **there are NO shortcuts. NONE.**

What is it about thicker shag pile carpets that these people feel is worth causing someone else pain. The ruined reputation and having to look over your shoulder will last a whole lot longer than any money they have ripped off.

But there are people out there who give themselves a handsome living at the expense often of people who can ill afford it.

However, if it hadn't have been for this situation, I may never have met Debbie. Remember, she assisted me through my toughest of times in recent history, so things happen for a reason. Every time.

Debbie didn't need to buy a licence to gain the success she currently enjoys. She just needed a jolt and two years' business experience under her belt.

I've been guilty in the past of being whipped up into a frenzy that some third party's product or service would rapidly accelerate my company's growth.

And so was Paul Sinclair @VirtualSinclair of the now Bristol-based company Virtually There. He shared a great example of this.

Back in the 90s he had a business called Sinclair Associates, which is now no longer.

He knew he needed appointments, so after spending an afternoon researching telemarketing companies, he decided to approach one that had a nice posh office and an impressive client list on its brochure.

After a couple of meetings, he appointed them to undertake a one-week campaign.

Hundreds of calls later.

Net result was a spreadsheet filed, full of calls completed and an invoice for thousands.

Real business. No.

The document was formatted nicely though.

He knew there was a market for his service, so he thought he'd come at it from a different perspective. Seeking out a local hotel, he personally created a database of 750 local businesses, and then mailed each of them inviting them to a **Free Lunchtime Seminar**. As we know there is no such thing as a free lunch and Paul had to stump up the cash for the food and venue.

Net result – a room full of warm leads as 25 people turn up. Paul presented to them and offered a free psychometric test to each of the attendees whilst they tucked into their free lunch.

What he took away from this whole exercise is that the problem with cold calling is you ring someone up to tell them they've got an itch when they haven't.

With the free lunch approach, only those with an itch turn up.

From a mail-shot of 750, 25 turned up, from which he converted 30% on the day to paying clients.

He used the free lunchtime seminar for over 15 years all across the UK. Always successful, with excellent ROI.

Others in his industry started to do similar but he thinks it is still an excellent way . . . especially when the product or service is hard to explain/demonstrate. That's low investment, high impact. Right there.

As time goes on, your reputation will build and then one day you'll get a call. That's just how it is. The longer you stay in the game, the more opportunities that just find you. My call was from Radio 2's Jeremy Vine show, asking if I would like to go live that day and debate some business issue. I was so excited, seven million listeners!

I was in such a tizz that I immediately jumped into action, calling our website host and spent a few hundred pounds increasing our bandwidth, as I just knew that this would have a massive impact on the business – the exposure would be monumental.

As you do when you're *that* certain of something.

The show broadcast live and I beat my nerves. I got out of the studio and logged onto my website to see how many extra users we had gained.

Not a single one. No noticeable change to web traffic whatsoever.

I've been on the show loads of times since that first appearance. I've learned since that day that there is no magic bullet that suddenly spikes your business, apart from I'm reliably informed, if you get it right on *Dragon's Den*.

So I no longer waste time running around trying to increase bandwidth. Experience is good like that. It saves you time and money. One of my little tricks that has served me well is always being busy. As in, just before going into a meeting, I'll always be scheduled to make a phone call (whether I am or not), otherwise I can end up with my time being eaten up with "dicking about" by proxy. At the start of a call, look at your watch, 14:50, and then say from the outset to the person you are speaking to that you have another call to do at 15:00.

This hones your thinking. You end up getting the call done and achieving the same outcome as if you had left the end time open. Difference is you've saved 10 minutes here, 20 minutes there. The cumulative effect of doing this is that it frees up masses of your time and money to do other stuff.

Recall every mistake. Remember every time it didn't go your way. You've already paid the price of every experience learned. Now is the time to turn them to your advantage. Each drop you file away is like a down payment which will save you time, money, anxiety in the future.

Business takes time. If you haven't got time, you haven't got a business.

So what have you learned?

LIFE:

BUSINESS:

IDEAS:

Is your life/business likely to be that little bit easier? Y / N

14

SUN WILL SHINE

Take a big breath in . . . smell that?

It's air, it's oxygen, it means . . .

Be thankful.

You are alive.

From this moment on, start loving your life. Start loving who you are, your strengths and weaknesses. You are unique.

One in a million. In fact if my biology teacher is to be believed, one in 80 billion!

I sound like a pothead hippy writing that . . .

Stop feeling like you have to conform to others' templates of what your business/life should be or how your thoughts should be shaped.

It's all you.

If you are happy with your life and you are not hurting anyone, enjoy.

If you are unhappy with your life and hurting yourself, do something about it.

You can, you know.

So what are you going to do with it, the rest of your life?

What part of your legacy are you going to leave with today?

Tell yourself right now. Speak to your subconscious, the drivers in that brain of yours.

Tell them where you would like to be heading for the remainder of your days.

Remember when I talked earlier about Health, Wealth and Realth and about one of them being out of kilter and hoping the one that is the weakest is your wealth? You need to recognise that money is not the be all and end all of life, nor in fact is business success. The truth about life is that you most likely already have the real things in life that are important, yet somehow you forgot that in pursuit of a Rado watch.

No question, money is important. But the trick is getting it for a price that isn't too costly.

What good is having loads of money if you are unhappy or poorly?

On your journey towards business success, look after yourself. Without you, there is no business success.

Sick-cess – got a successful business, but you're ill.

Great. Instead of buying that watch, spend the money on private healthcare. Oh and get a will as the last time I checked death had a 100% success rate.

Your direction may have changed as a result of reading this book, or maybe it's confirmed that the path you are now on is the right one.

Either way, that's good.

Everything in your life is a reflection of a choice you have made. If you want a different life, make different choices.

Make each today count. Soldiers are drilled day in, day out. They know that in the event of a sniper attack, you'll go left, I'll go right and we'll lay down suppressing fire.

They sometimes train with live ammo.

Then when the day comes and they are out in the field and a sniper attacks, they are not hiding behind a tree shaking uncontrollably. They know what the hell to do.

You are going to have to drill yourself. Know that in the event of any situation, you are not going to crumble. You are going to use every fibre, every adversity, every experience of your life to work out what to do.

The answer is within. Yes it is. Right now, you can do this. You can do pretty much anything.

Stuff you have no control over, stop worrying about it. It doesn't serve you.

Keep positive. Don't flap. Don't panic. Stick to your loose plan, but be prepared to adapt it.

Accept that sometimes things don't go your way. It's going to be OK. You are going to be OK. Accept that you are not perfect. Accept that to get to C, you've got to go via A and B but most people quit during the A to B bit.

Say what you are going to do, and do it.

I met a banker, a heavyweight one. He would like me to share his story with you. He makes around £2 million a year, he drives the best 911 Porsche money can buy. It's true, I've been in it. A supremely handsome man, when he was a 30-something, he looked straight out of a Diet Coke advert, married with a couple of kids.

Things didn't work out with his marriage.

Probably a bit *too handsome.*

He left his wife and his children. It got messy, family courts and everything, net result was he wouldn't be seeing his kids anytime soon.

He said to me, "I thought as soon as they got old enough, the kids would make the decision to want to see me again".

It didn't pan out that way. The now teenagers want nothing to do with the man that walked out on them.

He's now 40, still on his £2 million a year. Still driving a new Porsche. But the 911 his money can't buy is being there on all those birthdays of his two lads.

The very thing that he worked so hard for, he no longer has.

Ten years on. He is broken. Has a hole in his heart.

Still.

I've been asked not to reveal his identity and I will of course respect that, but he wanted his story to help others avoid similar self-destruction. I think everyone reading this will also respect the life lesson here and I feel it's really brave of him to have shared this with us, in the hope that someone else may avoid a similar outcome.

Be careful of the things YOU take for granted.

It's rare in life that you can have both your cake and eat it, forever. Something has to give. Fellas, save 69p, if you want Angry Birds for free, simply tell your wife that you are having an affair.

Aussie Roy is back.

It's all just junk. Look around you at all that stuff. Junk. Any man who's been divorced can tell you that even when it all gets taken off you, life goes on – it's definitely not the end of the world. Spend your money on experiences, helping others, developing yourself – all these things can never be taken off you. It's you who earned and acquired all that stuff. You can do it all again tomorrow. It's not what life is all about. In business, by all means collaborate, work together, help each other and take on bigger projects with the help of allies. But keep the lines of separation open!

There are many ways to collaborate – subcontract, share profits through invoices, swap jobs, employees, ideas and work under each other. There's no need to "get married"! Don't form bigger companies, make people directors, or hop into bed with your business partners. It often ends the same way a marriage does! With people getting taken advantage of, and expensive divorce proceedings, so always leave a graceful exit open.

Roy's just got divorced and clearly not bitter and scarred whatsoever! Joking, but he has run a highly successful engineering company for the last 30 years and it's always fascinating digging into his well of experience. We do pursue stuff that we don't really need. Stuff. We swap life for stuff. Do you really need shag pile carpet so thick that you have to fit a fluorescent flag on your cat's tail? Why do you need a top of the range Aga cooker in order to cook those Findus 100% Crispy Beef Pancakes?

Never forget your achievements.

@Crockersaurus

"Write down your Top Ten achievements. Read them frequently. Never forget what you have achieved.

Your current situation might be significantly different but you still have the skills and the attitude for success.

Running a workshop for those facing redundancy, I asked them to complete a short exercise by jotting down their greatest achievements. Some people went straight to it, while others thought about it for a bit and then started writing.

One guy was just staring at the paper. I tried to help him but he couldn't think of any achievements in his 25-year career. I encouraged him to think outside work. He continued to stare at the paper. Then suddenly a HUGE smile came to his face. "I caught a 41 pound carp once!"

I asked him what skills he had used to catch that carp.

He immediately gave me a list of many skills that would be essential for him to bounce back from the situation he was facing. He was better equipped than many of those around him.

Life. Business. Just got easier.

I do wish @Crockersaurus would tweet more! Love that, he is absolutely right. We've all achieved so much, so use that to spur you on.

When you keep getting knocked on your arse, money is not a big enough reason or motivator to keep getting up. So think about why you are doing it and what the money is going to be used for.

My driving force to keep going, every time I didn't feel like doing so, was to take my kids to Disney in Florida. I made that promise to them.

I'm sat here, writing this final chapter and my four-year-old lad, Brandon, walks into my home office and tries to sit on my knee. I say, "Stinky (my nickname for him), Daddy has to finish his work to earn some pennies son".

He ignored me and kept on with his attempt at sitting on my knee.

I'm now typing this, laughing to myself, with my youngest sat on my knee.

That's what the whole premise of this book is all about.

Finding the time for those who are most important to you. Yet, even I forgot my own lesson, it's easily done. I'm human. We are never going to get it perfect, but as long as we're aiming that's good enough.

I just had five minutes of cuddles and chatting about absolute nothing, like four year olds do and then, like a Dickensian street urchin, he nicked my iPad and scurried off into another room, where he is probably on YouTube, as I can now hear the *SpongeBob* theme tune playing. You know what life is about.

It's about having a cheeky scoot on a supermarket shopping trolley, when no else is looking. If you really want to be radical in this world, do it when someone is watching.

It's about driving through big puddles in your car – I never get tired of that.

It's about feeding the ducks, followed by pebble skimming competitions with your kids. And letting them win.

Before you change the world, you may have to change yourself. Work every day to close the gap between where you are now, and where you want to be.

Right now, you can do pretty much whatever (legally) you want to. There is no one stopping you, nor do you need permission.

How will you be remembered?

"It's OK for you though Brad, with your big network."

Was it OK for me – when I got shot at, at 21?

When I did years on the dole, from the age of 23?

When I was addicted to drugs at 27?

When I delivered pizzas at 32?

When I had a nervous breakdown at 39?

You could hold onto those things which have happened to you along the way and use them as the reason as to why your life isn't where you would like it to be.

Or do what I did – when I hit 30 I decided to move on and to change direction.

You have one life. Do something positive with it.

Your life is not mapped out by anyone or anything.

There is still time to avoid *your* caterpillar cake.

Everyone is good at something. Be ambitious, but not at the expense of derailing your life.

Personal self-belief is one of the biggest factors in preventing people from being happy or taking risks, and winning at life is being happy with who you are. You are the only person that has observed your whole life, known your every thought and seen your every victory and defeat. You know your strengths, your weaknesses and motivations behind your every move and your past decisions will be still affecting your life.

Next time you look in the mirror, remind yourself of your life mission.

Stay away from the haters, critics and blamers. Find your support with the dreamers, thinkers and doers.

You are truly the only person that knows who you are and what, if you were to give it your all, you can achieve. A life without problems does not exist. Life is imperfect, occasionally complicated, but very few problems are insurmountable.

Find your new enthusiasm and gain a clearer mind. Get your mind right and you'll get your business right. And I promise you this – your life, your business, *will* just get easier.

So what have you learned?

LIFE:

BUSINESS:

IDEAS:

Is your life/business likely to be that little bit easier? Y / N

Life. Business. Just got easier.

About Brad Burton

1973, born, Salford, Dad left, primary school, computer games, role-playing games, class clown, no qualifications, shop boy, BMX bikes, girls, chalet cleaner, night clubbing, pothead, more girls, games journalist, Dad, shot at, moved away, depressed, dole, more pot, shop manager, blagged CV head of marketing, dole, director,

Jonathon Jacob @jjacobphoto
www.jjacobphotography.co.uk

Oxford sucked, dole, three days away from bankruptcy, father again, depressed, maisonette above a chippy, married, employed, shove job up arse, self-employed, depression, skint, skint, skint, whinging wife, author, Dad again, stopped smoking pot, 4Networking, bluffing, struggling, speaking, still skint, skint, skint, Dad, 5,000+ events a year, uh oh, keynote speaker, bought dream Range Rover Sport, still waiting to be found out, sold dream Range Rover Sport, author again, people are buying them, scratches head, burned out, near divorce, crisis averted, just, snapped up by top publisher for third book, still waiting to be found out. 150 word bio. Get in!

@BradBurton

BOOM.

Business Blah Blah Blah

www.BradBurton.biz – Find out more about me and the various ways I can work with you, your people, your business, all in one funky place.

www.4Networking.biz – I'm MD of 4Networking, a truly unique approach to business networking, fun, unstuffy, yet effective.

Members can attend any of our 5,000+ events all over the UK each year.

At each meeting you have 3 × 10-minute one-to-one meetings with other attendees.

It's a fresh way of doing business the British way and works beautifully for businesses of all sizes and types.

I'M NOT AS THICK AS I LOOK.

Acknowledgements

All the following in some way gave me the mental strength . . .

@4NTerryCooper "I don't use Twitter enough".

@bigjohnraine Seven years and not out.

@BradsPA PAs should never have to hear their boss crying.

@BradsMate "No retreat. No surrender".

@debbiehuxton "Are you willing to risk it all?"

@dannymatharu "Would you let a lodger steal your house?"

@FitnessJai "/@BradBurton".

@IWantAPoem "My number 1 fan". Probably.

@Just_Dee_X "Boobies".

@LexiconMarketing Subbing and stuff my end.

@MarkyMedia "Jenga/LOLS".

@Marketing_Jen "We're gonna need a bigger table".

@MissDalley Sound, sound advice and sound friend.

@NikkiHesford Sometimes just being there helps.

@NoRedBraces "You got this . . ."/Gum-shield in.

@PointandStare The Alf Garnett of 4Networking.

@PRMira My constant groupie/cheerleader.

@RachelElnaugh "You are a FIRE TORNADO Brad".

@richardjeaton   "Team winning".

@ScottHider   Final round corner man.

@shaawasmund   "We don't spend enough time together".

@TLC_Tom   "We've all been there".

@TRIGGASDC   "Sun Will Shine . . .".

@YansTheMan   "That morning helped give me focus".

Roy "G'Day mate" Hurley

@markbrimson/@TheNickElston/@MrKimHambley/
@IamTheCarFinder   LYM

@nickfiddz/@StuartYoules/@vinniemarsh   "Curry rocks".

@4nhq   And all those 4Networking team and members.

And everyone who in some way contributed to this book.
Thanks.

. . . and encouragement to keep going.

As a result of a tweet of mine, the following three businesses each donated £££ to the family of @DetectiveDenise and I promised I would include each of them in my next book.

Show them some Twitter love.

@Dinalli   I build insanely great apps. It's my dream. I owe it to myself to never give up on that.

@Rob_Terry_1

@ChaseKeepsBooks